Marine Corps
Warfighting
Publication
MCWP 6-10

Leading Marines

January 2019

US Marine Corps

United States Government

PCN 143 000129 00

DEPARTMENT OF THE NAVY
Headquarters United States Marine Corps
Washington, D.C. 20380-1775

FOREWORD

Since our 30th Commandant, General Carl E. Mundy, first published *Leading Marines* in 1995, it's had a positive impact throughout our Marine Corps. It's generated spirited discussions about what it means to be a Marine, and how to lead Marines, and it is the base document for the leadership curriculum in all our resident schools. Our philosophy of leadership, as described in this publication, is in consonance with our rich and storied past.

That said, it was time to update *Leading Marines*. As Marines, we lead by example, often instilling values using stories. During the last 13 years of continuous combat, Marines have added to our legacy, some of their stories superbly illustrating our leadership philosophy. You'll recognize many of those stories herein. We speak in this publication about those timeless attributes that form the soul of our Corps . . . those attributes that carried Marines forward through the wheat fields of Belleau Wood to the strongholds of Fallujah and Marjah. Additionally, our core values, leadership traits, and leadership principles are given added emphasis in this edition. In the end, the intent of this revision is to better describe our timeless leadership philosophy. It was in this spirit that *Leading Marines* was revised.

Simply put, this publication describes the leadership philosophy that distinguishes the U.S. Marine Corps. This publication is not meant to be a "how to" guide on leadership, rather, it provides broad guidance in the form of concepts and values.

Additionally, *Leading Marines* is not designed as a reference manual; it is meant to be read from cover to cover. Its three chapters have a natural progression. Chapter 1 describes our ethos—who we are and what we do for our Nation. Building on that understanding, Chapter 2 covers the foundations of Marine Corps leadership. Chapter 3 then addresses overcoming the challenges our leaders face.

Once you read this publication, I charge you to discuss it with your peers, subordinates, and seniors. As General Mundy laid out in his foreword to the original publication in 1995, leading Marines is the most important responsibility in our Corps, and thus we must educate the heart and mind to prevail on the battlefield and in the barracks, in war and in peace.

Semper Fidelis,

JAMES F. AMOS
General, U.S. Marine Corps
Commandant of the Marine Corps

Publication Control Number: 143 000129 00

Leading Marines

Introduction

The act of leading Marines is a sacred responsibility and a rewarding experience. This publication describes a leadership philosophy that speaks to **who we are** as Marines. It is about the relationship between the leader and the led. It is also about the bond between all Marines that is formed in the common forge of selfless service and shared hardships. It's in this forge where Marines are hardened like steel, and the undefinable spirit that forms the character of our Corps is born. It draws from shared experiences, hardships, and challenges in training and combat.

Leading Marines is not meant to be read passively; as you read this publication, think about the material. You should reflect on, discuss, and apply the concepts presented in this publication. Furthermore, it is the responsibility of leaders at all levels to mentor and develop the next generation of Marine leaders. This publication contains numerous vignettes, drawn from our rich history, to give substance to the concepts. Marine leaders should add to these examples by sharing their own experiences with their Marines.

To effectively lead Marines, you must first understand what it is to be a Marine; you need to know **who we are** and **what we do** for our Nation. Our core values and traditions lie at the heart of our Marine Corps ethos and form the basis of the first chapter. The second chapter focuses on the foundations of Marine Corps leadership—the relationship between the leader and the led and the leadership traits and principles that are taught to every

Marine. It goes on to address morale, discipline, and courage. The third chapter describes some of the challenges to leading in uncertain conditions and how to overcome them. It relies on the stories of Marines to illustrate our character and vividly depict, through action, what is required to lead Marines.

In the end, this publication speaks about the soul of our Corps, leadership, and its many attributes. It's written about Marines, and it's written for Marines.

Chapter 1

Our Ethos

Resolved, that two Battalions of [M]arines be raised . . . that particular care be taken that no persons be appointed to office or [e]nlisted into said Battalions, but such as are good seamen, or so acquainted with maritime affairs as to be able to serve to advantage by sea, when required. . . . That they be distinguished by the names of the first and second battalions of American Marines . . .[1]

—Resolution of the Continental Congress on 10 November 1775

Among Marines there is a fierce loyalty to the Corps that persists long after the uniform is in mothballs. . . . Woven through that sense of belonging, like a steel thread, is an elitist spirit. Marines are convinced that, being few in number, they are selective, better, and, above all, different.[2]

—Lieutenant General Victor H. Krulak

Before there was a United States, there was a Marine Corps. The Marine Corps legacy began with a resolution of the Continental Congress on 10 November 1775 and continues through today. Our predecessors passed down the rich heritage that shaped each succeeding generation of Marines.

Knowing who we are as Marines is essential to understanding how we lead Marines. Marines come from all walks of life, but being a Marine transcends our differences. Being a Marine is not a job or a particular occupational specialty. It is a calling. It is a state of mind. Being a Marine comes from the eagle, globe, and anchor tattooed on the soul of every one who has worn our cloth. It is a mark seared in our innermost being that comes after the rite of passage in boot camp at Parris Island or San Diego, or initial officer training at Quantico—when young men and women earn the title "Marine." Once they undergo the transformation, they become a Marine for life.

The story of Michael "Mike" Joseph Mansfield illustrates the lifelong impact of the Marine Corps. At age 14 during World War I, he dropped out of school, lied about his age, and enlisted in the US Navy. After discovering his real age, the Navy discharged him. He then served as a private in the US Army from 1919 to 1920. Afterwards, he joined the Marines where he served from 1920 to 1922, stateside and in the Philippines. In 1942, he began a distinguished career in politics with his election to the US House of Representatives, representing Montana's 1st Congressional District. After serving five terms in the House of Representatives, the voters elected him to the US Senate where he eventually rose to the position of Senate Majority Leader. He retired from the Senate in 1976. From 1977 to 1988, he served as the US Ambassador to Japan. At age 98, he passed away and was laid to rest in Arlington National Cemetery. One would expect his grave to be marked by an imposing monument recording his military, congressional, and ambassadorial service. Instead, his common headstone, shared by many interred in Arlington, simply reads: "Michael Joseph Mansfield PVT US Marine Corps MAR 16 1903 OCT 5 2001." At the end of Mike Mansfield's life, being a Marine was all that mattered. The story of Private Mansfield illustrates what we mean when we say, "Once a Marine, always a Marine."

The final resting place of Private Michael Mansfield, US Marine Corps, Arlington National Cemetery.

Being a Marine is being part of something larger than oneself. There is a spirit—an *esprit*—that defines our Corps. To understand what it means to be a Marine, you must understand how we make Marines by instilling and abiding by the core values of honor, courage, and commitment. As a Marine leader, you must also understand our naval character and expeditionary mindset, our philosophy that every Marine is a rifleman, and our commitment to selfless service, all of which are in keeping with Marine tradition.

MAKING MARINES: THE TRANSFORMATION

A sense of elitism has grown ". . . from the fact that every Marine, whether enlisted or officer, goes through the same training experience. Both the training of recruits and the basic education of officers—going back to 1805—have endowed the Corps with a sense of cohesiveness enjoyed by no other American service."[3]

Every Service recruits young men and women from American society. The difference with the Marines is that we don't rely on bonuses and benefits to attract the best. We offer a challenge. We ask, "Do you have what it takes to be a Marine?" Not, "What can the Marine Corps do for you?" We then send those who accept the challenge to Parris Island, San Diego, or Quantico where they receive more than just superb training; they are ingrained with a shared sense of service, honor, and discipline. The result is remarkable. Those who have what it takes undergo a personal transformation so incredible that often parents have difficulty recognizing their children who become Marines. A mother of a Marine described it this way:

> When my son left home he had no motivation, he was lazy, slobby, no pride, no self-worth. This is the boy that got off the bus March 18th at Parris Island. The man that I met on Thursday for [parents'] day is AWESOME. There is no way I can describe to you all the difference. He looks different, he walks different, he talks different, he has such a sense of bearing and pride all I could do was look at him in awe. Oh yes, the training is hard, what he went through is unimaginable to any one that has not been there. They are definitely taught to be Warriors. Let me tell you the surprise of what else they are taught. My Marine son has better values, better morals, better manners than [anyone] I know. It is so much more than Yes Sir, Yes [Ma'am] . . . so much more. He cares about how he looks, he cares about what he does, and [it's] not a boastful, bad ass thing. He is a true gentleman. I saw patience, and a calmness in him that I have never seen. I could never express my gratitude enough to the Marine Corps for what they have given my son.[4]

Those who make it through boot camp and initial officer training win our Nation's battles and return to society better citizens. The Corps' history is full of tales of individual triumphs—Sergeant Major Dan Daly, Gunnery Sergeant John Basilone, Lieutenant General "Chesty" Puller, Colonel John Glenn, Private First Class

James Anderson, Jr., Corporal Jason Dunham, Sergeant Dakota Meyer, Corporal Kyle Carpenter, and countless others—that exhibit the indomitable spirit of Marines in combat and in surmounting day-to-day challenges. You, as a Marine leader, have the responsibility to sustain the transformation.

OUR CORE VALUES

Our motto is *Semper Fidelis*, Always Faithful. We are faithful to our Nation, the Corps, and to each other. This is not blind faith, it is a faith guided by our values. As Marines, we share the core values of **honor**, **courage**, and **commitment**. As much as anything else, our core values set us apart. They give us strength, influence our attitudes, and regulate our behavior. They bond all Marines into a band of brothers that can meet any challenge. In the end, these values make us better citizens when we return to a society that sometimes questions values. Many Marines realize this when they go home for the first time and notice they are different from their old buddies.

HONOR: The bedrock of our character. The quality that guides Marines to exemplify the ultimate in ethical and moral behavior; never to lie, cheat, or steal; to abide by an uncompromising concept of integrity; to respect human dignity; to have concern for each other. The quality of maturity, dedication, trust, and dependability that commits Marines to act responsibly, to be accountable for actions, to fulfill obligations, and to hold others accountable for their actions.

COURAGE: The heart of our core values. Courage is the mental, moral, and physical strength the Corps ingrains in Marines to carry them through the challenges of combat and the mastery of fear, to do what is right in every situation, to adhere to a higher standard of personal conduct, to lead by example, and to make tough decisions under pressure. It is the inner strength that enables Marines to take that extra step.

COMMITMENT: The spirit of determination and dedication in Marines that leads to professionalism and mastery of the art of war. It leads to the highest order of discipline for unit and self; it is the ingredient that enables 24-hour-a-day dedication to Corps and Country, pride, concern for others, and an unrelenting determination to achieve a standard of excellence in every endeavor. Commitment is the value that establishes the Marine as the warrior and citizen others strive to emulate.

It takes time for Marines to internalize these values and it is a leader's responsibility to live them, demonstrate them, and instill them in their subordinates.

OUR NAVAL CHARACTER AND EXPEDITIONARY MINDSET

Ours is a world ideally suited for the employment of warriors who come from the sea, whose past and potential future battlegrounds are mainly in the "watery maze," green water, and coastal regions that comprise the littorals of the world. Operations along these littorals require special "training and preparation . . . along Marine Corps lines. It is not enough that the troops be skilled infantry men or artillery men . . . they must be skilled water men and jungle men who know it can be done—Marines with Marine training."[5]

The Marine Corps' naval character has shaped the Corps since its inception. Our naval character makes us different because it combines the characteristics of soldiers and sailors. In 1775, Congress resolved that two battalions of Marines be raised ". . . such as are good seamen, or so acquainted with maritime affairs as to be able to serve to advantage at sea, when required."[6] The result is a sea soldier—an odd conglomeration that talks like one, dresses like another, and fights better than both. The determination to be different, and remain different, manifested itself in many ways over the years—from military appearance, to strict obedience to orders, to disciplined behavior, to adherence to standards, to persistent engaged leadership, and, most of all, to an unyielding conviction that we exist to fight. These characteristics have distinguished Marines since 1775.

The historic partnership between the Navy and the Marine Corps is a heritage that continues today. The anchor in our emblem symbolizes that the individual Marine remains a soldier of the sea. Marine officers are "naval" officers and our pilots are "naval" aviators. Marines have served on ships since our inception, and the Marine Corps has been part of the Department of the Navy since 1834.

As early as 1798, the Secretary of the Navy noted that the Corps' missions were of an "amphibious nature." Though early Marines served primarily on board ships as part of the ship's company, they always had a secondary role to serve as expeditionary forces, whenever or wherever needed. Marine Captain Samuel Nicholas' amphibious expedition to New Providence island in the Bahamas in 1776 and Marine Lieutenant Presley O'Bannon's 1804 landing in Tripoli were the first deployments of American forces on foreign soil. Since then, Marines have conducted expeditionary and sustained operations ashore in Cuba, Panama, the Philippines, Haiti, China, France, the Pacific, Korea, Lebanon, the Dominican Republic, Vietnam, Grenada, Kuwait, Afghanistan, Iraq, and scores of other places.

Although specific missions differ, what remains constant is our unyielding commitment to protect the lives of our citizens and the

Marines landing on New Providence.

interests of the United States. Our purpose, mandated by Congress, is to be the Nation's signature crisis response force. As such, we "must be most ready when the Nation . . . is least ready."[7] As you read this, there are Marines stationed overseas and forward deployed. Some are guarding embassies, others are afloat, and still others are conducting operations ashore. To Marines, being expeditionary is more than the mere ability to deploy overseas when needed. It is an institutional imperative that drives us to deploy rapidly and operate on arrival. Often deploying into an austere environment, Marines bring what they need to accomplish the mission and often that means they are ready to fight. This expeditionary mindset is the most critical contributor to the Corps' success in crisis response and complex contingencies. Marine leaders have deliberately cultivated this mindset for generations. It is this mindset that generates both

Marines of Company F, 2d Battalion, 4th Marines resting between combat operations in Helmand Province, Afghanistan.

combat power and the organizational flexibility to accomplish diverse missions around the world. Our expeditionary culture emphasizes being fast, austere, and lethal.

EVERY MARINE A RIFLEMAN

> "THE DEADLIEST WEAPON IN THE WORLD IS A **MARINE AND HIS RIFLE.**"[8]
>
> —*General John "Black Jack" Pershing, US Army*

Our role as an expeditionary force in readiness requires that we make every Marine a rifleman first. Before we teach Marines to fly aircraft, drive tanks, maintain equipment, or any of the other skills necessary for a combat ready Marine Corps, we teach them to shoot accurately. Then we teach them basic infantry skills. During expeditionary operations, no Marine is very far from the fighting; there are no "rear area Marines." Combat and combat service support units defend themselves and, when necessary, fight as provisional infantry.

Every Marine a rifleman is not a new concept. The first Marine aviator to earn the Medal of Honor in World War II, Captain Henry "Hank" Elrod, was a fighter pilot with VMF-211. He arrived on Wake Island on 4 December 1941 and 4 days later he was fighting the Japanese in the air. On 12 December, he single-handedly attacked a flight of 22 enemy planes, downing 2 of them. Additionally, he executed several low-altitude bombing and strafing runs on enemy ships. During one of these attacks, he sank the Japanese destroyer *Kisaragi*. When hostile fire eventually destroyed all US aircraft on Wake Island, he assumed command of part of the ground defense. In this role, he was responsible in large measure for the strength of his sector's gallant resistance as he and his Marines valiantly repulsed numerous Japanese attacks. On 23 December, Captain Elrod was mortally wounded while protecting his men who were carrying ammunition to a gun emplacement.[9]

Nearly 71 years later, Marines from the same squadron (redesignated VMA-211) would once again prove that every Marine is a rifleman. On the night of 14 September 2012, 15 heavily-armed Taliban insurgents dressed in US Army uniforms breached the eastern perimeter of Camp Bastion in Helmand Province, Afghanistan. The insurgents split into three teams of five each and commenced a coordinated attack on the airfield. Realizing the flight line was under attack, the VMA-211 commander, Lieutenant Colonel Christopher Raible, armed only with his pistol, organized his pinned down Marines into fire teams for a counterattack. During the fighting, he was mortally wounded when a rocket propelled grenade detonated next to him.[10]

During the attack on the airfield, Sergeant Bradley Atwell, an avionics technician, immediately directed his Marines to grab their rifles and accompany him. Leading his Marines, Sergeant Atwell ran toward the aircraft and structural fires that were visible along the flight line, as tracer rounds ricocheted between him and the other Marines. "While continuing to press forward along the edge of the aircraft parking area, [he] became separated from the others when a rocket propelled grenade exploded approximately 3 meters from his position, knocking him down with mortal injuries. Sergeant Atwell crawled to cover and returned fire in the direction of the enemy until succumbing to his wounds."[11]

Meanwhile, the squadron executive officer, Major Robb T. McDonald, and two other officers maneuvered more than a mile on foot through an area exposed to enemy fire. When his commanding officer was mortally wounded, Major McDonald took command. While leading a small team to reconnoiter the flight line, he killed an insurgent with a rifle he had borrowed and then expertly coordinated two helicopter strikes. Additionally, Marines from another squadron, VMM-161, killed one group of five insurgents with small arms fire as the enemy tried to advance along the flight line. In the end, the enemy was defeated after a 4-hour firefight by Marine aviators and maintainers, personnel from No. 51 Squadron Royal Air Force Regiment, and helicopter fire support.[12]

Marines fighting as riflemen occur with such regularity that non-Marines are often surprised to learn that there are any specialties in the Corps other than infantry. This perception is part of what makes the Corps exceptional.

SELFLESSNESS

Another element that defines Marines is selflessness: a spirit that subordinates self-interest to that of the Country, Corps, and fellow Marines. There is almost nothing more precious to a Marine than a fellow Marine. This traditional bond flows from the rigorous training that all Marines receive and the shared danger and adversity inherent in combat operations. William Manchester described his World War II experience as a Marine fighting in the Pacific this way, "Those men on the line were my family, my home. They were closer to me than I can say, closer than any friends had been or ever would be. They had never let me down, and I couldn't do it to them. I had to be with them, rather than let them die and me live with the knowledge that I might have saved them. Men, I now knew, do not fight for flag or country, for the Marine Corps or glory or any other abstraction. They fight for one another. Any man in combat who lacks comrades who will die for him, or for whom he is willing to die, is not a man at all. He is truly damned."[13]

In one of the many fights en route to the Chosin Reservoir during the Korean War, Private Stanley Robinson lay wounded in a warming tent of the medical battalion and listened "to the cascading sound of a fire fight to the north. It was not long before the ambulance jeeps drew up outside. Litterbearers brought in a stretcher and placed it alongside Robinson.

> "What outfit you from?" Robinson asked.
> "Easy, 7th," the inert figure mumbled.
> "Did we get hit?"

"Clobbered. Mr. Yancey's wounded—so's the skipper—everybody is, I guess."

Robinson sat up. In the darkness he got into his clothes and parka. He stifled a moan as he pulled the shoe-pacs on over his swollen feet.

"Be seein' you, Mac," he whispered.

Robinson stumbled to the entrance and lurched through the opening. The cold night air made him gasp. He was selecting a weapon from a discarded stack of rifles when a corpsman came to him.

"What'n hell you doin', Robinson?"

"What does it look like, Doc?" . . . Robinson slung the rifle over his shoulder and headed for the hill mass to the north. When he came to the steep hillside he had to crawl. The blisters on his feet had broken and his socks were wet with blood and pus. Robinson found his way to Easy Company, he found Yancey.

"What'n hell you doin' here?" Yancey asked hoarsely.

"Looking for a job."

Yancey spat blood in the snow. "You got one. Over there."[14]

Marines understand why there was no emotional greeting from Yancey when Robinson rejoined the platoon. Thanks were neither expected nor given. Both knew Private Robinson would rejoin his fellow Marines, if he could. Private Robinson's action in 1950 captures the essence of selfless service. Leaving the warming tent, selecting a weapon, and struggling to rejoin his battered platoon was an act of extraordinary personal courage, but it was not an aberration; instead, it was an act that sprang from the rich tradition of Marines who choose service over self.

Fifty-four years later, First Sergeant Bradley Kasal clearly demonstrated selfless service as the Weapons Company First Sergeant, 3d Battalion, 1st Marines during the Battle of Fallujah. On 13 November 2004, First Sergeant Kasal was assisting 1st Section, Combined Anti-Armor Team (CAAT) Platoon, in providing a traveling overwatch for 3d Squad, 3d Platoon, Company K, while they cleared in zone:

> During the clearing operation, 3d Squad along with the CAAT squad heard a large volume of fire and observed wounded members of an adjacent platoon rapidly exiting a building to their immediate front. They quickly learned that Marines were pinned down in the house by an unknown number of insurgents. Realizing that they were short personnel to make an entry and clear the structure, the 3d Squad Leader asked the CAAT squad if they could assist with clearing the building. Without hesitation, First Sergeant Kasal volunteered. He led the squad into the house, suppressing and killing the enemy, who were fighting from hardened positions. After the first room was cleared, First Sergeant Kasal and two other Marines observed a wounded Marine two rooms away from their position. Upon entry into the first of the two rooms, First Sergeant Kasal immediately confronted, engaged, and killed an insurgent. Continuing towards the wounded Marine, the three Marines received heavy enemy fire as soon as they entered the second room. First Sergeant Kasal

and another Marine were both struck in the legs becoming urgent casualties. The enemy began throwing grenades on the wounded Marines below. Selflessly, First Sergeant Kasal rolled on top of the other Marine in order to shield him. After reinforcements arrived, First Sergeant Kasal, with seven gunshot and five fragmentation wounds, refused aid until the other Marines were extracted. A total of seven wounded men were medically evacuated from the building before First Sergeant Kasal.[15]

Despite his grievous wounds, First Sergeant Kasal continued to shout words of encouragement to his Marines while he engaged the enemy. Later as First Sergeant Kasal was put into the CASEVAC [casualty evacuation] helicopter, he grabbed his battalion commander by the flak jacket and implored him to take care of the

From left to right: Lance Corporal Christopher Marquez, First Sergeant Bradley Kasal, and Lance Corporal Dan Shaeffer in Fallujah 2004. (Photo courtesy of photographer Lucian Read.)

Marines. First Sergeant Kasal could have remained outside of the building, coordinating support and the medical evacuation. Instead, he chose to face the enemy alongside his Marines.

Private Robinson and First Sergeant Kasal epitomize the Marine ethos of selfless service, which Marines continue to demonstrate in countless ways and in countless places. It is a part of who we are.

Marine Traditions

> *There is nothing particularly glorious about sweaty fellows going along to fight. And yet they represent a great deal more than individuals mustered into a division. There is something behind those men: the old battles, long forgotten, that secured our [N]ation . . . traditions of things endured, and things accomplished such as regiments hand down forever . . .*[16]
>
> —Captain John W. Thomason, Jr.

Marine traditions are an inseparable part of who we are as Marines. Ordinary men and women, who showed extraordinary leadership and courage, both physical and moral, shaped and continue to shape our heritage. Separately and collectively, our traditions set us apart from other fighting forces and are the cement that bonds the Marine Corps together and give Marines a common outlook regardless of rank, unit, or billet. Our traditions transcend the individual and are shared by all Marines.

Marines believe they should be where the fight is. In 1983, a veteran of the terrorist bombing in Beirut stood amidst the rubble, carnage, and despair surrounding his fallen comrades, barraged by questions from news reporters. "Should you be here? Should anyone be here? Should the United States pull out?" The young lance corporal's answer was straightforward: "Where else should I be? I'm a United States Marine. If anyone must be here, it should be Marines."

Lance Corporal Jeffrey Nashton was gravely wounded—unable to talk or see—during the Beirut bombing and was evacuated to a hospital in Germany. While in the hospital, he was visited by the Commandant. As General P. X. Kelley stooped beside the Marine

Aftermath of Beirut bombing.

to say a few words of comfort into his ear, the lance corporal reached up to feel the stars to make sure that the man talking to him was who he claimed to be. Unable to see or speak, weak from a concussion and other injuries, the young Marine motioned for something with which to write. He could have written anything; he could have asked for anything. Instead, he wrote, "*Semper Fi*"—Always Faithful. He was concerned more about his Corps and his fellow Marines than himself.[17]

Individual Marines—like those described above—feed our Corps' spirit. From their first day of training to their first assignments, to their first celebration of the Marine Corps birthday, the Corps infuses those who set out to be Marines with an understanding of the deeds of their predecessors. The spirit of the Marine Corps is sustained as today's Marines step forward to take their place. These Marines give meaning to the phrases "*Semper Fidelis*," "uncommon valor," "every Marine a rifleman," and "first to fight."

Marine traditions manifest themselves in other ways as well. Our language reflects our naval heritage, while our birthday, hymn, and uniforms set the Corps apart from other military services.

Much of our distinct language comes from our naval roots. Marines refer to bathrooms as heads, floors as decks, ceilings as overheads, walls as bulkheads, and corridors as passageways. We respond to verbal orders with "Aye, Aye, Sir," acknowledging that we both understand and will comply with the command. Other terms are also steeped in lore. The term "Leatherneck" comes from the stiff leather collar worn by Marines from 1798 to 1872. Legend has it that German soldiers referred to the Marines at Belleau Wood as *Teufelhunden,* that led to the nickname Devil Dogs, which remains in use today.[18]

Every Marine knows the birth date of the Corps. November 10th is a day of celebration and reflection for all Marines in and out of uniform. For some, the day is celebrated with a special meal, the cutting of a cake, and the reading of Major General Lejeune's message as part of a birthday ball. For others, the day is marked with the cutting of an MRE pound cake with a Ka-Bar fighting knife during a lull in the action. And for still others, it's phone calls to former squad mates to wish them "Happy Birthday, Marine."

Marines in Korea celebrate the Marine Corps 176th birthday.
On a shell-scarred ridge in eastern Korea, battle weary veterans of the 1st Marine Division take time out to cut the cake celebrating their 176th birthday on 10 November. No cake knife being available, the Leathernecks fell back on the trusty bayonet to slice the ceremonial cake. Complete with frosting and the Marine Corps emblem, cakes were delivered to every Leatherneck unit in Korea on the historic occasion.

Among the five Armed Services of our Nation, four have Service *songs*; only the Marine Corps has a *hymn*. Long before it became fashionable to stand for all Service songs, Marines always stood when the hymn was played. To this day, while others stand with cheers and applause to their Service song, Marines stand quietly, unwaveringly at attention, as the hymn of their Corps is played. There is a physical and emotional reaction as the *Marines' Hymn* is played or sung—the back straightens, the chest swells, shoulders move rearward, and a tingle runs along a Marine's spine—because *Marines are different.*

A moment in time at the Chosin Reservoir is a testament to the power of the *Marines' Hymn.* "The 1st Marine Division, fighting its way back from the Chosin Reservoir in December 1950, was embattled amid the snows from the moment the column struck its camp at Hagaru [*sic*]. By midnight, after heavy loss through the day, it had bivouacked at Kotori [*sic*], still surrounded, still far from the sea. [The commanding general] was alone in his tent. It was his [worst] moment. The task ahead seemed hopeless. Suddenly he heard music. Outside some [Marines, on their way to a warming tent] were singing the *Marines' Hymn.* 'All doubt left me,' said [the general]. 'I knew then we had it made.'"[19]

Our uniforms are also rich in history and tradition. Marine officers still carry the Mameluke sword, which the governor of Derna, Tripoli presented to Lieutenant Presley O'Bannon in 1805. Our NCOs carry the next oldest weapon in our inventory, the Marine Corps noncommissioned officer's sword, which dates back to 1850. Of course, there is no more distinctive uniform than Dress Blues.

From the quatrefoil on the officer's cover to the eagle, globe, and anchor on the collar to the blood stripes on the trousers, Dress Blues are steeped in history. It is not just the uniforms themselves that set Marines apart; it is the proud and disciplined manner in which we wear them. Commandant L. F. Chapman received a letter from a friend of the Corps; the letter described, as well as anyone could, the importance Marines place on their uniform and in setting the example:

> Recently I was in an air terminal. Most military people there presented a pretty sloppy appearance—coats unbuttoned, ties loosened, etc. There was a Marine corporal in uniform who was just the opposite. I spoke to the Marine and pointed out the difference to him. I asked him why it was so. His answer was: "The Marines don't do that."[20]

Whether it is our language, birthday, hymn, or uniform, Marine Corps traditions run deep. They are an integral part of who we are.

Knowing who we are and what we represent is essential to understanding how we lead Marines.

This Page Intentionally Left Blank

Chapter 2

Foundations of Leadership

Leaders must have a strong sense of the great responsibility of their office; the resources they will expend in war are human lives.[1]

—MCDP 1, *Warfighting*

The following excerpt from Marine Corps Order No. 29, published 14 August 1920, applies to all Marine Corps leaders and remains true today. It also provides an excellent framework to describe Marine Corps leadership.

> Young Marines respond quickly and readily to the exhibition of qualities of leadership on the part of their officers. Each officer must endeavor by all means in his power to develop within himself those qualities of leadership, including industry, justice, self-control, unselfishness, honor, and courage, which will fit him to be a real leader of men and which will aid in establishing the relationship described below. . . .
>
> . . . The relation between officers and enlisted men should in no sense be that of superior and inferior nor that of master and servant, but rather that of teacher and scholar. In fact, it should partake of the nature of the relation between father and son, to the extent that officers, especially commanders, are responsible for the physical, mental, and moral welfare, as well as the discipline and military training of the men under their command who are serving the Nation in the Marine Corps. . . .The provisions of the above apply generally to the relationships of non-commissioned officers with their subordinates and apply specifically to non-commissioned officers who may be exercising command authority.[2]
>
> –Major General John A. Lejeune

THE RELATIONSHIP BETWEEN LEADERS AND THEIR MARINES

Take a moment to reflect on how Major General Lejeune describes the relationship between leaders and their Marines. Just like a parent, Marine leaders "are responsible for the physical, mental, and moral welfare"[3] of those in their charge. They are justifiably proud when their Marines succeed and they help them up when they fall short. This type of relationship requires Marine Corps leaders to engage their Marines. Leaders care for and know their Marines. They sacrifice for those in their charge, which is why leaders take care of their Marines' needs before their own. Observe an act as basic as hot chow being served in the field and you'll see the junior Marines eating first, followed by the NCOs, SNCOs, and finally the officers. Marine leaders take care of their Marines' physical, mental, and spiritual needs. They also care about the well-being and professional and personal development of their Marines. The leaders' responsibilities extend to the families as well. Additionally, leaders know their Marines: where they're from, their upbringing, what's going on in their lives, their goals in life, their strengths, and their weaknesses.

Leaders of Marines assume an awesome responsibility that requires preparation. First, leaders must be of good character as defined by our core values and leadership traits. Second, leaders must learn and understand how to lead by applying the leadership principles. Third, leaders learn through experience—both their own experiences and the lessons learned from the experiences of those who came before.

LEADERSHIP TRAITS

Effective Marine Corps leaders possess certain character traits. Developing character begins in boot camp and basic officer training and continues throughout a Marine's career. The development of Marine Corps leaders builds upon our core values with 14 time-tested leadership traits. Memorizing the leadership traits using the memory aid JJ DID TIE BUCKLE is just the beginning. Good leaders develop and sustain these traits in themselves and their Marines, and these traits bear directly on the quality of our leadership. Each trait is important, and the lack of development in one or more of the traits makes for imbalanced and ineffective leaders.

Leaders who possess the trait of justice gain the trust and respect of subordinates by displaying fairness and impartiality. Leaders display judgment by making sound decisions. Dependable leaders can be counted on to carry out an assigned task. Leaders show initiative by adapting when the situation changes. Decisive leaders give orders clearly, forcefully, and promptly. Tactful leaders treat everyone with respect and courtesy and possess the ability to handle difficult situations with respect and decorum. Leaders embody integrity by being truthful and honest. Leaders build enthusiasm by displaying exuberance in the performance of their duties. Marines with good bearing look, talk, and act like leaders. Unselfish leaders take care of their Marines first. Courageous leaders do what is right despite physical danger or potential criticism. Knowledgeable leaders are technically and tactically proficient. Loyal leaders, guided by Marine Corps core values, are faithful to their Country, Corps, unit, seniors, peers, and subordinates.

Finally, leaders who possess both the physical and mental stamina to withstand pain, fatigue, stress, and hardship will endure. Embodiment of these traits allows Marines to lead with honor under trying circumstances.

2-5

LEADERSHIP PRINCIPLES

Marine Corps Leadership Principles

Be technically and tactically proficient
Know yourself and seek self-improvement
Know your Marines and look out for their welfare
Keep your Marines informed
Set the example
Ensure the task is understood, supervised, and accomplished
Train your Marines as a team
Make sound and timely decisions
Develop a sense of responsibility among your subordinates
Employ your unit in accordance with its capabilities
Seek responsibility and take responsibility for your actions

Good character is not enough to lead Marines. Men and women of character must learn how to lead. In addition to character, Marine leaders are guided by 11 leadership principles. They are generally self-explanatory; however, to truly understand these principles, leaders should discuss them through the use of ethical and tactical decision exercises, vignettes, and sea stories. Once understood, effective leaders apply the principles.

Morale

Morale is the natural result of a Marine's confidence in himself/herself, fellow Marines, and leaders. Major General Lejeune wrote, "Morale is three-fold—physical, mental or professional, and spiritual."[4] Leaders instill this confidence by developing the physical, mental, and spiritual readiness of their Marines along with the *esprit de corps* of their unit.

The goal of physical readiness is to develop the strength and endurance necessary to prevail in combat. Leaders must ensure their Marines are functionally fit to carry out their duties whether they are carrying heavy loads over rugged terrain, lifting artillery shells, loading bombs on aircraft, or stacking supplies on a truck. Strength alone is not enough. Marines must develop the endurance to perform these tasks over and over again with little sleep and in the extreme heat of tropics or the brutal cold of the mountains. Marines who are not up to the physical challenge become a burden on their fellow Marines.

The relationship between physical and mental endurance is well known. There are countless examples of Marines continuing beyond the point of physical exhaustion because they had the mental will to persevere. Many close battles have been lost when a commander concludes that he or she is defeated; those who persevere, win. Anxiety and fear of the unknown are the enemies of mental readiness. Leaders can combat these psychological enemies by keeping their Marines informed. The mind deals better with the known, no matter how horrible, than with the unknown. Mental readiness also includes the ability to make sound, timely decisions despite being tired, hungry, or afraid. Professional education and reading combined with stressful, realistic training are critical to building the mental experience that leaders can use to recognize patterns, see similarities between experience and new situations, and make rapid decisions in ambiguous situations.

The third component of morale is spiritual readiness, which is the resilience to meet the demands of Marine Corps service and the harsh reality of combat. Every man and woman possesses a spiritual reservoir. It is from this reservoir that we draw strength in the face of difficulty. In combat, Marines face privation, uncertainty, fear, and death. Outside of combat, Marines also face personal stressors, often compounded by deployments and family separation. Marines must replenish their spiritual reservoir from time to time, because when the reservoir runs dry, Marines break. That is the point where Marines freeze up, withdraw, become apathetic, and feel hopeless. Marine leaders must watch their Marines for signs of spiritual depletion and ensure they replenish their reservoir. Lieutenant Colonel Dave Grossman referred to it this way:

> One key characteristic of a great military leader is an ability to draw from the tremendous depths of fortitude within his

> own well, and in doing so he is fortifying his own men by permitting them to draw from his well. Many writers have recorded this process as being at work in the combat situations they observed. Lord Moran noted that "a few men had the stuff of leadership in them, they were like rafts to which all the rest of humanity clung for support and hope." Victory and success in battle also replenish individual and collective wells.[5]

Realistic training and frank discussions prepare Marines for the stress of combat and strengthen their emotional shock absorbers. The Commanding Officer, 3d Battalion, 5th Marines, Lieutenant Colonel Patrick J. Malay, understood the importance of realistic training. In preparation for his battalion's return to Iraq, he partnered with a local movie studio to provide his Marines with realistic training consisting of the use of authentic role players, special effects mimicking the dust and noise of explosions, blood packs on amputees, and the physical sting of simunitions. This immersive, realistic, and stressful training conditioned the Marines of 3d Battalion, 5th Marines to the stressors of combat and contributed to their success during the Battle for Fallujah in November 2004.

Major General Lejeune wrote that "Esprit de corps and morale are kindred subjects."[6] As leaders develop the individual Marine's physical, mental, and spiritual components of morale, leaders must also develop the unit's *esprit de corps*—the common spirit that bonds all members of a unit. Leaders develop this sense of camaraderie and purpose by instilling in their Marines a deep regard for the unit's history, traditions, and honor. *Esprit de corps* expresses the unit's will to fight and win in spite of seemingly insurmountable odds. This unit *esprit* and fighting spirit were demonstrated by the 1st Marine Division during November and December 1950.

> Surrounded and under tremendous pressure in the Chosin Reservoir area, the Division was ordered to withdraw, which began the epic battle against the bulk of the Chinese Third Route Army. The Division gallantly fought its way successively to Hagaru-ri, Koto-ri, Chinhung-ni, and Hamhung over twisting, mountainous, and icy roads in subzero temperatures. The Marines battled desperately night and day in the face of almost insurmountable odds throughout a period of two weeks of intense and sustained combat. The 1st Marine Division, Reinforced, defeated seven enemy divisions, together with elements of three others, inflicting major losses which seriously impaired the military effectiveness of the hostile forces for a considerable period of time. What is truly impressive is the Division emerged from its ordeal as a fighting unit, bringing out its wounded, its guns and equipment, and its prisoners.[7] One observer from President Truman's White House, an Army major general, reported that ". . . the Marine Corps was everything it claimed as a force in readiness. 'The First Marine Division is the most efficient and courageous combat unit I have ever seen or heard of.' "[8]

Nothing stops the Marines as they march south from Koto-ri, fighting their way through Chinese Communist hordes in subzero weather of the mountains. Despite their ordeal, these Marines hold their heads high.

Discipline

Marine Corps discipline is the state of order and obedience resulting from training. Discipline is not a collection of regulations, punishments, or a state of subservience. It is not blind obedience. Discipline is the execution of orders resulting from intelligent, willing obedience rather than obedience based solely upon habit or fear. Good leaders know that intelligent and willing obedience to orders often depends on Marines understanding the "why" of those orders. That is not to say that leaders always have the luxury of time to explain the intent to their Marines. When time permits, however, it is always prudent to explain the purpose of an order, because when Marines know why they are doing something, they are more committed and can adapt to changing circumstances. Habit also plays a part in discipline, which is why training includes immediate action drills, close order drill, and gun drills. Additionally, punishment for breaches of discipline is sometimes necessary, but only when good order and discipline demand it.

Leaders are responsible for the discipline necessary to produce orderly, coordinated action, which triumphs over the fear, fog, and friction of battle. Well-disciplined units perform well in combat. Conversely, poorly disciplined units suffer in combat. The experience of Colonel John Ripley in Vietnam illustrated that "really bad units were the ones that lost magazines. My battalion had to relieve a battalion at Con Thien because they ran out of magazines. We lost Marines doing that. My Marines were lost because another battalion had such poor discipline—losing their magazines."[9]

The key to discipline is establishing and maintaining standards. Every disciplined thing we do in training relates to combat effectiveness whether it is not smoking at night, cleaning our weapons when they need it, wearing ballistic eyewear, maintaining accountability, being aware of our geometry of fires, or treating our enemy's dead with respect. When setting a standard, leaders should also explain the purpose of the standard. For example, simply telling a Marine to shave forces a Marine to mindlessly maintain a standard and put shaving in the same category as painting rocks. So what could shaving possibly have to do with combat effectiveness? First, shaving fosters good hygiene, which is critical in combat. Lack of hygiene leads to illness; a Marine suffering from a high fever and diarrhea loses combat effectiveness. Second, a Marine's professional appearance—backed by our formidable reputation—instills fear in our enemies and confidence in those we protect. Third, shaving is an act of discipline that keeps Marines behaving like Marines. Colonel Ripley described it this way: "You're constantly on them to behave like Marines and like human beings. It's easy to drift off. For example, my men shaved once a day, every day, even on very limited water (though water was rarely a problem). Shaving marked the day, and it also marked us. It was a clean start to the day."[10]

Volumes have been written about combat leadership and discipline, but Marines most often practice leadership and discipline in garrison, in training, and in the barracks. It is before combat that leaders establish and inculcate standards. The Commanding Officer of 3d Battalion, 4th Marines, Lieutenant Colonel Bryan P. McCoy, communicated clear standards of discipline to his Marines prior to the invasion of Iraq in 2003. The textbox on the following page contains the section on discipline from his expectations of combat leaders that he used when talking to his leaders to ensure they clearly understood his intent.

Discipline

Do not allow graffiti on uniforms, do-rags, wristbands, or other forms of jackassery, period.

Pre-Combat Checks and Inspections and Post-Combat Checks and Inspections are SOP [standing operating procedures] and are at the *very heart* of leadership. This is a *basic habit*. They are called Pre-Combat Checks and Inspections for a reason; they are not Pre-Combat questions and assumptions. Leaders at the squad level carry out Checks and Inspections; platoon commanders and platoon sergeants verify—*no exceptions*.

Prescribed Load: Allow no deviations from the prescribed load and basic uniform—*ever*. Deviations are conscious decisions by a commanding officer based on analysis of the situation, *not* personal whims. At a minimum, Marines and Sailors will have their gas mask and weapons on their bodies *at all times*.

Helmets, when worn, will have the chinstrap on the chin; otherwise, it will not stay on when needed most. Allowing a Marine to wear a helmet without a chinstrap is making the Marine wear useless weight on his head and is a leadership failure.

Communications discipline: Enforce proper reporting and communications procedure. Use of "pro-words" (standardized radio jargon), reporting formats, and proper radio checks cut down on traffic and confusion.

Light discipline: Will be strictly enforced. Use of flashlights in the open, smoking and vehicle headlights from dusk to dawn is a commanding officer's decision, not one of personal convenience. We have Night Vision Devices (NVDs); use them. There is seldom a reason to break light discipline.

Hygiene discipline: Disease will cause casualties and rob units of combat power faster than the enemy could ever hope to do. Prior to eating chow in the field, squad leaders will inspect their squads for proper hygiene, clean hands, clean weapons, and the prescribed uniforms. Poor hygiene will rob us of combat power. All Marines and Sailors will perform hygiene every day, shaving, and brushing teeth at a minimum, with periodic foot inspections by leaders. Hand washing is mandatory and monitored. Leaders at the squad level check; platoon commanders and platoon sergeants verify— *no exceptions*.[11]

The combat success of 3d Battalion, 4th Marines fighting from Kuwait to Baghdad during Operation Iraqi Freedom was due in no small measure to the standards set and maintained both prior to and after crossing the line of departure. Discipline has been essential to success in combat throughout the Corps' history. Our NCOs are critical to maintaining discipline. In 1960, Corporal Gary Cooper described it this way:

> [I]f effective leadership is evident and functioning, we are strong and ready. If we are well disciplined, of high morale, possess an unquenchable unit spirit, and are efficient, we are the best in the business.
>
> Strive to create discipline in yourself and your Marines. Encourage high morale, foster esprit, and train for efficiency. You may never win the Medal of Honor, you may never be cited for your outstanding example, but you will have an inner satisfaction that comes only to those [who] give their all. Then, if you listen carefully . . . you will hear the voices of all the other good Marines who have gone before whisper the greatest commendation of them all—"Well done, Marine."[12]

Marine leaders strive to develop self-discipline in their Marines. Self-disciplined Marines are those who exercise self-control and take personal responsibility. They subordinate personal considerations such as convenience and comfort to do the right thing. Self-disciplined Marines do the right thing when no one is looking and they maintain their discipline because their fellow Marines are counting on them.

SETTING THE EXAMPLE

In a letter to the officers of the Marine Corps, Major General Lejeune wrote:[13]

> *You should never forget the power of example. The young men serving as enlisted men take their cue from you. If you conduct yourselves at all times as officers and gentlemen should conduct themselves, the moral tone of the whole Corps will be raised, its reputation, which is most precious to all of us, will be enhanced, and the esteem and affection in which the Corps is held by the American people will be increased. . .*
>
> *Let each one of us resolve to show in himself a good example of virtue, honor, patriotism, and subordination and to do all in his power, not only to maintain, but to increase the prestige, the efficiency, and the esprit of the grand old Corps to which we belong.*
>
> *With my best wishes for your success and happiness, I am, as always,*
>
> *Your sincere friend,*
>
> John A. Lejeune
>
> *Major General Commandant*

To instill self-discipline, Marines lead through personal example. In that way, their Marines know what right looks like. Disciplined Marines treat each other with dignity and respect. They do not perpetuate or condone harassment, hazing, or sexual assault. Setting a personal example requires "high moral standards reflecting virtue, honor, patriotism, and subordination in personal behavior and in performance."[14] These are inner qualities that mark leaders. Rather than outward marks of greatness, they are often deeply buried, and, in many cases, one must look closely to see an individual's inner strengths. Consider how Major General Lejeune described Medal of Honor recipient Sergeant Major John H. Quick: "Perhaps of all the Marines I ever knew, Quick approached more nearly the perfect type of noncommissioned officer. A calm, forceful, intelligent, loyal and courageous man he was. I never knew him to raise his voice, lose his temper, or use profane language, and yet he exacted and obtained prompt and explicit obedience from all persons subject to his orders."[15]

From left to right: Captain F.H. Delano, Sergeant Major John Quick, Lieutenant Colonel Wendall Neville, Colonel John Lejeune, and Major Smedley Butler in Vera Cruz, Mexico. (Photo courtesy of MCU Archives.)

Leading by example is inspirational. Consider the actions of First Lieutenant William D. Hawkins at Tarawa, on 20 November 1943:

> The first one off the landing craft, First Lieutenant Hawkins unhesitatingly moved forward under heavy enemy fire at the end of the Betio Pier, neutralizing enemy emplacements, allowing his Marines to assault the main beach positions. He fearlessly led his men as they fought desperately to gain a beachhead. Throughout the day and night, he repeatedly risked his life to direct and lead attacks on bunkers with grenades and demolitions. At dawn the next day, he continued clearing the beachhead of Japanese resistance, personally initiating an assault on a hostile position fortified by five enemy machine guns. Crawling forward under withering fire, he fired point-blank into the firing ports and completed the destruction with grenades. Refusing to withdraw after being seriously wounded in the chest during this skirmish, he destroyed three more pillboxes be-fore he was caught in a burst of Japanese shellfire and mortally wounded.[16]

First Lieutenant William Hawkins.

Although First Lieutenant Hawkins was gone, his scout-sniper platoon continued their deadly work clearing out enemy bunkers. He inspired his Marines to carry on without him. They were well-trained, well-led, and believed in each other and their cause. Of First Lieutenant Hawkins, the assault commander said, "It's not often that you can credit a first lieutenant with winning a battle, but Hawkins came as near to it as any man could. He was truly an inspiration."

TAKING CHARGE

It is not enough, however, that Marine leaders set the example. Their followers must be equally aware of the importance of following established standards. Followers are the backbone of any effective organization because without loyal, dedicated followers there can be no effective leaders. As one leader put it, "Every Marine, from the Commandant down, is a follower. The good followers, those who may be depended on to carry out their instructions precisely, without regard to difficulty, hazard, or personal risk, are the substance of the Corps. And where combat circumstance, as it often does, suddenly thrust upon the follower the responsibilities of a leader, those who are properly indoctrinated seize the opportunity and succeed."[17]

Corporal James Barrett's actions demonstrate clearly how the follower's and the leader's responsibilities merge. While Corporal

Barrett served as a squad leader with Company I, 3d Battalion, 26th Marines in the Republic of Vietnam, his "company came under heavy mortar, rocket, and artillery fire followed by a supported infantry assault by a numerically superior North Vietnamese Army force. In the initial attack, numerous casualties were taken and the company was forced to withdraw to a more advantageous position. Undaunted, Corporal Barrett courageously maintained his squad's position and directed accurate counter fire against the hordes of assaulting enemy. Assuming control of the platoon when his platoon commander became a casualty, he rallied his men, reorganized the platoon and led them in an effective counterattack against the enemy. With complete disregard for his own safety, he moved from position to position, encouraging his men and resupplying them with ammunition. Unhesitatingly, he aided the wounded and directed their evacuation. During the 6-hour ordeal, he repositioned his men five times to thwart the enemy advance and inflicted numerous casualties on the enemy force."[18]

Another corporal's actions with Embedded Training Team 2-8 (ETT 2-8) in Afghanistan further demonstrate how follower's and leader's responsibilities merge. On 8 September 2009, ETT 2-8 was on a mission to meet with the village elders of Ganjgal. Major Kevin Williams commanded the ETT and organized his unit into four elements: an observation post, a quick-reaction force, a dismounted patrol, and a security element at the objective rally point. Corporal Dakota Meyer was part of the security element at the objective rally point:

> Just after dawn, the dismounted patrol began moving up the winding 1-mile track to the village. Around 0530, the element

led by First Lieutenant Michael Johnson came under intense small arms and rocket propelled grenade (RPG) fire, trapping them in a U-shaped kill zone. Major Williams' element also came under intense fire. From the overwatch position, Corporal Steven Norman repeatedly attempted to suppress the enemy, which drew machine gun and RPG fire from multiple directions. Realizing the situation was rapidly deteriorating, Corporal Meyer and Staff Sergeant Juan Rodriguez-Chavez repeatedly asked permission to enter the kill zone, but they were denied in an effort to prevent more people from becoming trapped in the ambush. Finally, with First Lieutenant Johnson and his Marines no longer responding to radio calls, Staff Sergeant Rodriguez-Chavez and Corporal Meyer decided to act.

Corporal Meyer, despite being junior in rank, naturally assumed the role of vehicle commander in the vehicle's turret, directing Staff Sergeant Rodriguez-Chavez around obstacles and toward US and Afghan troops pinned down in the kill zone. Without regard for the intense enemy fire directed at them, Corporal Meyer killed a number of enemy fighters, some at near point blank range, as he and his driver made repeated trips into the ambush area.

During the first two trips, they pulled out two dozen Afghan soldiers, many of whom were wounded. When his Mk-19 became inoperable, Corporal Meyer directed a return to the rally point to switch to another gun-truck with a functional .50-caliber machine gun for a third trip into the ambush area where he provided fires to support the remaining US personnel and Afghan soldiers fighting their way out of the ambush. Despite a shrapnel wound to his arm, Corporal Meyer made two more trips into the ambush area accompanied by four other Afghan vehicles to recover more wounded Afghan soldiers and search for the missing US team members. On the fifth trip under heavy enemy fire, he dismounted and moved on foot to locate and recover the bodies of his team members. For their actions, Corporal Meyer received the Medal of Honor and Staff Sergeant Rodriguez-Chavez received the Navy Cross.[19]

Corporal Dakota Meyer.

PHYSICAL COURAGE

"Since war is a violent enterprise, danger is ever present. Since war is a human phenomenon, fear, the human reaction to danger, has a significant impact on the conduct of war. Everybody feels fear. Fear contributes to the corrosion of will. Leaders must foster the courage to overcome fear, both individually and within the unit. Courage is not the absence of fear; rather, it is the strength to overcome fear."[20] Physical courage is the mastery of the fear of death, bodily harm, or pain. Marines overcome our natural fear of injury and death and fight for three chief reasons: (1) we are well-trained and well-led, (2) we have convictions that will sustain us to the last sacrifice, and (3) we fight for one another.[21] The actions of Corporal Jason L. Dunham, Lance Corporal Kyle Carpenter, and Sergeant Barbara O. Barnwell are just three examples that represent countless displays of physical courage throughout our history.

Corporal Jason L. Dunham was born on 10 November 1981, so it is not surprising that he was destined to become a Marine.

> On 14 April 2004, Corporal Dunham's squad was conducting a reconnaissance mission in the town of Karabilah, Iraq, when they heard rocket propelled grenade and small arms fire erupt approximately 2 kilometers to the west. Without hesitation, he led his Combined Anti-Armor Team toward the engagement to provide fire support to their battalion commander's convoy, which had been ambushed as it was traveling to Camp Husaybah. The team quickly began to receive enemy fire. After dismounting, Corporal Dunham led one of his fire teams on foot several blocks south of the ambushed

convoy. Encountering seven Iraqi vehicles in a column attempting to depart, the team stopped the vehicles to search them for weapons. As the team approached the vehicles, an insurgent leaped out and attacked Corporal Dunham. Corporal Dunham wrestled the insurgent to the ground and, in the ensuing struggle, the insurgent released a grenade. Corporal Dunham immediately alerted his fellow Marines and without hesitation, he covered the grenade with his helmet and body, bearing the brunt of the explosion and shielding his Marines from the blast. In recognition of his selfless act of physical courage that saved the lives of at least two fellow Marines, Corporal Dunham received the Medal of Honor.[22]

Corporal Jason Dunham.

On 19 November 2010, a team of engineers, an interpreter, Afghan National Army personnel, and a squad from 3d Platoon, Company F, 2d Battalion, 9th Marines established Patrol Base Dakota in a small village in the hotly contested area of Marjah in Helmand Province, Afghanistan. Around 0900 on 21 November, Lance Corporal Kyle Carpenter and Lance Corporal Nicholas Eufrazio were manning an observation post atop the combat operations center when the enemy began engaging with sporadic small arms fire. In the ensuing hour, the enemy forces maneuvered close enough to the perimeter to throw three grenades over the compound wall. The first grenade exploded near the west entry point, wounding an Afghan soldier. The second grenade failed to detonate. The third landed on top of the combat operations center. Immediately recognizing the danger and with complete disregard for his personal safety, Lance Corporal Carpenter covered the grenade with his body and absorbed most of the blast. For his courageous and selfless act that left him grievously wounded and saved the life of Lance Corporal Eufrazio, Lance Corporal Carpenter received the Medal of Honor. [23]

Lance Corporal Kyle Carpenter and Lance Corporal Nicholas Eufrazio in Marjah, Afghanistan, during their 2010 deployment.

Displays of physical courage are not limited to combat. Sergeant Barbara Barnwell was on her 2-week reserve drill at Camp Lejeune in 1952. While swimming 100 to 150 yards offshore, she heard cries for help from a male Marine who was struggling in the heavy surf 50 feet from her. Without regard for her safety, Sergeant Barnwell quickly swam to the near-hysterical man and managed to secure a hold on him, despite the fact that he fought and scratched her and pulled her underwater several times. For 20 minutes, she battled both the Marine and a severe undercurrent as she courageously towed the man to shallow water where she was met by a lifeguard. They pulled the now unconscious man to the beach and administered artificial respiration. Once she realized the artificial respiration was successful, Sergeant Barnwell modestly left the scene without learning the identity of the man she had rescued. In recognition of her selfless act of physical courage, Sergeant Barnwell was the first woman to receive the Navy and Marine Corps Medal.[24]

General Lemuel Shepherd, Jr. presenting the Navy and Marine Corps Medal to Staff Sergeant Barbara Barnwell.

Moral courage

Moral courage is the mastery of the fear of social consequences such as being perceived as disloyal, alienation, ridicule, punishment, job loss, or loss of social status. The Marine Corps trains us to endure combat, violence, and death—along with other less arduous situations. It trains us to make life or death decisions over both our Marines and our enemies. In the end, the decisions we make must pass the test of ethical behavior, which often requires moral courage. Ethical choices often involve a moral dilemma: the necessity to choose between competing obligations in circumstances that prevent one from doing both. Moral courage compels us to make the right ethical decision in situations where the easiest or most expedient action fails to adhere to a higher standard of personal conduct.

Marines fight with, and for, honor, which means we adhere to defined standards of conduct no matter how hot, tired, or frustrated we may be. Imagine it is the summer of 2004 and you are part of a mounted patrol in Iraq. You are feeling the stress of the oppressive heat, lack of sleep, and an elusive enemy. Suddenly, you feel the thump of an explosion behind you. The patrol leader's voice crackles through the radio's speaker, directing the convoy to halt. Following the battle drill, you dismount and begin sweeping the field to your right, searching for the triggerman. With the temperature in excess of 100 degrees, the inside of your body armor feels like a furnace, your heart is racing, and you gasp for breath. You and two other Marines see a figure darting into a building. One of the Marines shouts that he/she is ready to engage. As the senior Marine in your group, you order the Marine to wait until there is positive identification. As the moments slowly pass, a frightened and clearly noncombatant woman emerges. At this point, you re-cross the field to join several other Marines who have detained the proprietor of a roadside stand. It is clear from the proximity of the stand and the abandoned sandal of someone fleeing the scene that the roadside stand's proprieter obviously knows who initiated the attack. Understanding what is right keeps you from physically attacking the liar and beating the proprieter until he/she tells you who triggered the improvised explosive device (IED). By exercising restraint, you retained your honor and set the example of moral courage for your Marines.

Marine leaders must also make difficult choices in peacetime. At times, these choices will place them in an unfavorable light with either subordinates or higher authority. It was standing operating procedure in Company A to award a 72-hour liberty to platoons that went 30 days with no disciplinary problems. Returning from a lengthy field exercise, 1st Platoon reached 28 days with no problems, only to have a Marine go UA [unauthorized absence] on the 29th. No one outside the platoon knew the Marine was missing. The platoon commander faced a moral dilemma: ignore the UA and ensure the Marines went on a well-earned liberty; or report the absence and forfeit liberty and, perhaps, the morale of the platoon. The platoon commander chose the latter and reported the UA to the company commander. The Marines were disappointed—not only at the loss of hard-earned liberty, but also, initially, in their leader. But slowly, over succeeding days, they came to respect the difficult choice made by the platoon commander. Soon, they came to realize that they could count on their leader to do what was right, no matter how difficult or unpopular. Moreover, the company commander realized there was a subordinate that could be trusted. Regardless of the circumstances, the Corps expects all Marines to make the ethically correct choice and to be held accountable for a failure to do so.

Even given the best training, how well Marines perform depends on the leadership and courage demonstrated by their leaders—their moral courage. A unit led by an able and aggressive leader who commands respect because he/she sets the example and demonstrated courage and confidence will perform any task asked of them.[25]

Marine leaders must be capable, on a moment's notice, of deploying literally anywhere and doing whatever must be done upon arrival—attacking, protecting, or assisting. Many times, Marines will have to make decisions, under the partial protection of a poncho, in the drizzle of an uncertain dawn, and without all the facts. In combat, decisions often must be immediate and instinctive. During those times, it will not always be possible to identify all the components of the problem and use a lengthy, logical problem-solving process to reach a decision. As such, the Marine Corps continues to prepare leaders of all ranks for this moment.

This Page Intentionally Left Blank

Chapter 3

Overcoming Challenges

An army that maintains its cohesion under the most murderous fire; that cannot be shaken by imaginary fears and resists well-founded ones with all its might; that, proud of its victories, will not lose the strength to obey orders and its respect and trust for its officers even in defeat; whose physical power, like the muscles of an athlete, has been steeled by training in privation and effort; a force that regards such efforts as a means to victory rather than a curse on its cause; that is mindful of all these duties and qualities by virtue of the single powerful idea of the honor of its arms—such an army is imbued with the true military spirit.[1]

—Carl von Clausewitz

Friction

Carl von Clausewitz wrote, "Everything in war is very simple, but the simplest thing is difficult. The difficulties accumulate and end by producing a kind of friction that is inconceivable unless one has experienced war."[2] Friction makes simple tasks hard, acts constantly to tear down the will of the individual Marine, and interferes with unit cohesion. It operates across the entire spectrum of conflict, from garrison activities to combat, from Marine air-ground task force command elements down to the most forward fighting position. Friction can be caused by external factors such as the physical environment, the nature of the mission, friendly decisions, or enemy action.

Inadequate or inaccurate intelligence also contributes to friction by causing uncertainty. This uncertainty is sometimes called the "fog of war," where things are not always what the leader expected. "This expression [fog of war] describes both the literal fog created by the dust, smoke, and debris of the battlefield, and more importantly the mental fog of confusion and uncertainty created by lack of knowledge of the enemy, the chaotic noise, mental and physical fatigue, and fear."[3]

The 1975 Cambodian seizure of the unarmed American container ship SS *Mayaguez*, and its subsequent recapture, is a classic example of what friction can do to leaders at all levels and its ultimate impact on ground forces. In this case, the rushed planning, convoluted command relationships, misleading intelligence, lack of joint procedures, and confused decisions created friction that cost the lives of Marines, Sailors, and Airmen.

Marines recapture the *Mayaguez*.

During the afternoon of 12 May 1975, Cambodian forces seized the *Mayaguez*. With the recent memory of the North Korean capture of the USS *Pueblo*, President Ford exercised a military option on 13 May. Although the Navy-Marine Corps forces that participated in the evacuation of Saigon 2 weeks earlier could have reconstituted in a matter of days, Commander-in-Chief Pacific Command (CINCPAC)[4] chose instead an *ad hoc* rapid response option consisting of readily available Marine ground forces supported by Air Force helicopters and close air support.

Intelligence throughout the operation was faulty. Although a US Navy P-3 surveillance aircraft tracked the *Mayaguez* to the island of Koh Tang where the ship anchored around noon on 13 May, US forces never pinpointed the location of the crew. Repeated requests for photographic reconnaissance were denied.

The *ad hoc* nature of the task organization was compounded by an odd selection of commanders. The CINCPAC designated US Air Force Lieutenant General Burns, Commander, 7th Air Force, as the on-scene commander and US Air Force Colonel Anders, Deputy Commander, 56th Special Operations Wing, as the operational task force commander. The Commanding General, III Marine Amphibious Force (III MAF), designated Colonel Johnson from the III MAF G-3 (a spare colonel awaiting PCS orders) as the Marine Task Group Commander; Lieutenant Colonel Austin, Commanding Officer, Battalion Landing Team (BLT) 2/9 as the Koh Tang raid commander; and Major Porter, Executive Officer, BLT 1/4 as the *Mayaguez* raid commander. Despite his title, Lieutenant General Burns was never actually on scene. Adding to the friction, distance and poor communications later cut Colonel Johnson and Lieutenant Colonel Austin out of the decisionmaking loop. That these commanders had neither trained together nor had habitual relationships was a continual source of friction throughout the operation.

The plan called for 57 Marines from Company D, 1st Battalion, 4th Marines, plus augments, to board and recapture the *Mayaguez*. Simultaneously, 8 US Air Force CH/HH-53 helicopters would land roughly 180 Marines from BLT 2/9 into two zones on Koh Tang to seize the island and rescue the crew.

The plan went awry as soon as the company commander and one of the squad leaders leapt from the USS *Holt* to the *Mayaguez*. After the first two jumped, the surge that resulted from the *Holt* coming alongside pushed the two ships apart. For the next 5 minutes or so, Captain Wood and Corporal Coker were the only two Marines on the hostile ship. Sailors on the *Holt* quickly threw over lines allowing the crew to lash the two ships together. More friction was generated by the senior level decision to saturate the *Mayaguez* with tear gas to incapacitate the expected Cambodian defenders. This "good idea" forced the boarding party to execute the difficult task of clearing the ship while wearing gas masks. The gas masks limited vision, increased exertion, and hampered communication; however, prior nuclear, biological, chemical training helped overcome some of the friction. To improve communication, the Marines lifted their masks, shouted orders, and then replaced and cleared their masks instead of relying solely on hand and arm signals. Fortunately for the Marines, the Cambodians had abandoned the *Mayaguez* earlier, which prevented the friction from becoming catastrophic. In the end, the Marines recaptured the deserted ship without firing a shot.

While the recapture of the *Mayaguez* was fortunately anticlimactic, the helicopter assault on Koh Tang, on the other hand, turned into a blood bath. Problems assaulting Koh Tang began in the planning phase. The intelligence available to Marine planners indicated there were 18 to 20 Cambodian irregulars on the island. Due to security procedures, higher headquarters did not provide the Marines with intelligence reports that estimated the enemy strength at 200 fighters armed with 82-mm mortars, 75-mm recoilless rifles, .30-caliber machine guns, and a rocket propelled grenade launcher. In addition to the incorrect intelligence, there were no tactical maps available. Overhead reconnaissance imagery would have mitigated that shortfall, which was requested by the 7th Fleet, but higher headquarters repeatedly denied the request until it was too late to process the film. In the end, the only reconnaissance available to the BLT commander was an Army U-21. However, the Air Force restricted the U-21's flight to a 6,000-foot altitude and the only camera onboard was a Marine's pocket camera. Despite these restrictions, Lieutenant Colonel Austin identified two sites during the flight that were clear enough for use as landing zones.

On 14 May around 0900, an Air Force F-4 pilot spotted and reported a fishing vessel with what appeared to be Caucasians aboard heading towards the Cambodian mainland. Despite this report, Lieutenant General Burns and his staff continued planning for operations on Koh Tang.

On 15 May, expecting little resistance, eight Air Force helicopters flew toward the island. The first two helicopters that approached the eastern landing zone were hit by enemy fire. One helicopter crashed in the ocean; killing the copilot, 10 Marines, and 2 corpsmen. The other helicopter crash landed on the beach. In the western landing zone, the first helicopter landed unopposed and the Marines exited the first aircraft, whereupon the enemy opened fire with small arms, rocket, and mortar fire. The damaged helicopter barely made it out of the zone before ditching in the ocean. From that point, the situation continued to deteriorate. After the insertion of the first wave, the Marines found themselves separated into three groups, struggling to coordinate their action.

Further complicating matters was the release of the *Mayaguez's* crew on the morning of 15 May. Concurrent with the launching of the second assault wave, the USS *Wilson* recovered the *Mayageuz's* crew from a Thai fishing boat. Upon learning of the recovery, authorities in Washington ordered an immediate cessation of offensive operations on Koh Tang. As a result, the airborne mission commander ordered the second assault wave to return to base. Desperate for reinforcement, the commander on the ground finally convinced Lieutenant General Burns to allow the second wave to land. For the rest of the day, the Marines worked through inter-Service friction to coordinate Air Force close air support missions and the Marines' withdrawal. By 2010 that evening, the last Marines to make it off the island lifted out of the landing zone. Several hours later, the Company E commander discovered three of his Marines were missing. The fates of Lance Corporal Joseph N. Hargrove, Private First Class Gary C. Hall, and Private Danny G. Marshall remain unknown. Additionally, the body of Lance Corporal Ashton N. Looney was unintentionally left on the beach. The cost of recovering the *Mayaguez* was 15 killed, 3 missing (later declared dead), and 49 wounded.[5]

Friction is inevitable and Marines must learn to deal with it; however, Marine leaders can minimize its effects. The *Mayaguez* incident makes it clear that senior leaders should establish command relationships that facilitate operations. Additionally, forces should be task-organized to take advantage of unit capabilities and habitual relationships. Senior leaders should also be aware of the effect of a "good idea," such as saturating a ship with tear gas, and the friction it induces into tactical operations. Finally, leaders at all levels can reduce friction through realistic training and rehearsals.

Among the many factors that cause friction, perhaps the moral and physical challenges to leading are the hardest to overcome. Together, they can produce obstacles that may prevent leaders and units from accomplishing their mission. Although they affect us in very different ways, the moral and physical elements cannot be separated. Moral factors play an important role in developing the physical capacity of individuals and units.

Moral Challenge

Leaders overcome moral challenges by exercising moral courage. As explained in Chapter 2, moral courage is the mastery of the fear of social consequences such as being perceived as disloyal, alienation, ridicule, punishment, job loss, or loss of social status. In some cases, the right choice is crystal clear. In other cases, the correct course of action is not so clear. In the end, leaders must always accept full responsibility for their actions. The following vignettes illustrate the actions of morally courageous leaders.

Gaining moral ascendancy requires that subordinates feel that their leaders genuinely care for them, that they are fighting for a worthy cause, and that their sacrifices are not made in vain. Acting as a buffer to protect subordinates is a key responsibility of any leader. Consider the actions of the Second Division's Commanding General, during World War I.

> One evening in November 1918, Major General Lejeune overheard one of his watch officers talking on the phone with higher headquarters. When queried, the watch officer told General Lejeune that Third Corps gave orders for Second Division to march the next morning. Knowing that his men where exhausted, he immediately got on the phone with the Third Corps staff officer. The staff officer told General Lejeune that Field Marshal Foch had directed the Second Division to begin the attack from Stenay, which required the Division to march 60 kilometers: 40 kilometers to cross the river at Dun-sur-Meuse and then 20 kilometers to Stenay. General Lejeune pointed out that the Division could cross at Pouilly, which would considerably reduce the marching distance. The staff officer countered that the Division could not cross there because it would require passage through German lines. General Lejeune then suggested the Division repair the bridge at Stenay, which would significantly reduce the length of the movement. The lieutenant colonel from Third Corps stated that he did not have the authority to change the order. When General Lejeune said that he would take it up with someone more senior, the staff officer replied that all the senior officers were asleep. General Lejeune then replied, "It is better to wake up one General than to have twenty-five thousand sick and exhausted men march sixty kilometers, and I will do so myself." In the end, Third Corps modified the

orders and the Division engineers repaired the bridge, saving many tired Marines and Soldiers unnecessary hardship.[6]

In another instance, this time in Vietnam, all that stood between the North Vietnamese Army 308th Division and Quang Tri Province was the bridge at Dong Ha, defended by a company of Vietnamese Marines. Realizing that the company would not be able to hold the bridge, the senior American advisor to the 3d ARVN Division (Forward), Lieutenant Colonel Gerald H. Turley, determined that the bridge had to be destroyed. The Deputy ARVN Division Commander would not give permission to destroy the bridge. Lieutenant Colonel Turley conferred with the VNMC Brigade 258 Commander who had local responsibility. The Brigade Commander said the decision would have to come from I Corps. Lieutenant Colonel Turley radioed the First Regional Assistance Command (FRAC) G-3 to gain permission. The FRAC G-3 denied permission and said permission would have to come from Saigon. Realizing the dire consequences of not taking action and knowing the career risk he was taking, Lieutenant Colonel Turley ordered Major James E. Smock, US Army, and Captain John W. Ripley, USMC, to blow the bridge. His decision to act prevented a regimental sized armor force from crossing the river, which blunted the North Vietnamese advance.[7]

The ancient philosopher Confucius phrased it this way, "To see what is right and not to do it is want of courage."[8] Moral courage is a private courage, a form of conscience that can often be an even tougher challenge than physical courage, especially in peacetime. It serves not only as a foundation of our leadership philosophy; it is also a challenge that Marine leaders must face every day. If Marines do not have the moral courage in peacetime to meet consistently the high standards and expectations of the Marine Corps, then they are not likely to have the moral courage to make the difficult decisions that may determine the outcome of a battle or a campaign.

The following vignette highlights that moral dilemmas often are about conflicting loyalties that cause Marines to delay doing the right thing. As leaders, we must resolve these internal battles quickly to arrive at the right decision and must not be blinded by misplaced loyalty. If these dilemmas were easy, it wouldn't be called moral courage.

Note: The following is based on a true story; the names have been changed to protect privacy.

Sergeant Parilla was a member of an Inspector-Instructor administrative section along with two other sergeants. One day, Sergeant Parilla complained to Sergeant Adkins that Sergeant Vickers had never run a unit diary entry in all of their time together. Sergeant Adkins replied that it was just as well, since Sergeant Vickers would probably run illegal entries on himself. Those remarks seemed odd to Sergeant Parilla, so he checked the record. He discovered Segeant Vickers entered basic allowance for housing (BAH) for San Francisco, CA, in the amount of $2,100 for himself, which was well over the BAH for their area which was

$780. Sergeant Vickers also backdated the entry, embezzling $15,840 from the United States Government.

Upon discovering Sergeant Vicker's transgression, Sergeant Parilla told Sergeant Adkins that he would personally confront Sergeant Vickers and tell the First Sergeant. Sergeant Adkins asked him not to report the false entries, because he had run falsified diary entries on himself. In fact, Sergeant Adkins had run family separation allowance on himself and backdated it two years, defrauding the United States Government of $6,000. Sergeant Parilla confronted the two sergeants. They told him not to worry and that no one would find out because they were about to get out of the Marine Corps. When Sergeant Parilla pushed the issue, the two sergeants threatened to kill him and later gave him $2,000 to keep quiet. He didn't want the money, but he took it to buy time to figure out what to do.

Sergeant Parilla was conflicted. These Marines were his buddies. They worked as a team, their families shared meals, and they often went hunting together. They shared tough times, to include conducting more than 100 funerals. They looked out for each other. Sergeant Adkins had a wife and a 1-week-old baby. Sergeant Vickers had a wife and two children. Growing up, Sergeant Parilla learned not to "rat out" his buddies. He wrestled with what he should do. He knew what the two Marines had done was wrong. If he did nothing, the theft would likely remain undetected. If he told his chain of command, then two wives and three children would suffer and his fellow Marines would think he was disloyal. He talked through these conflicting thoughts with his wife. Sergeant Parilla decided he needed to report the crimes, so he went for a drive to collect his thoughts and figure out how to tell his command.

In the meantime, his wife, concerned for her family's safety, called the training chief, Master Sergeant Powers, who immediately phoned Sergeant Parilla to confirm the facts. Together, they determined that calling the Naval Criminal Investigative Service was the best course of action. Agents arrested the two sergeants who were later court-martialed and sent to the brig. In the end, Sergeant Parilla realized that his loyalty belonged with the Marine Corps and his unit. By stealing, Sergeants Adkins and Vickers were the ones being disloyal.

Physical Challenge

The physical demands of battle encompass more than being fit and these demands influence both the leader and the led. The effects of sleep deprivation, poor diet, poor hygiene, and, most importantly, fear have to be understood and must be a part of training. No one is immune to fatigue. As Marines become increasingly tired, they often lose the ability to make sound, rapid decisions and are susceptible to being confused, disoriented, and ultimately ineffective. Guts, pride, and energy drinks are not substitutes for fitness. A leader must be fit to concentrate fully on the mission or task at hand.

The exact limits of endurance cannot be determined, but physical conditioning is one method of reducing the effects of fatigue, increasing self-confidence, and reducing stress. The physical development of Marine leaders must include dealing with the natural fear of violence, which contributes significantly to the fog and friction of combat. Units, and unit leaders, that do not have the mental and physical strength to overcome fear will not be able to fight effectively and overcome friction. Captain John Ripley's actions at Dong Ha vividly depict the physical demands sometimes placed on individuals.

Captain John Ripley's heroic action at the bridge at Dong Ha. (Photo courtesy of David Burnett/Contact Press Images.)

As you may recall from the moral challenge vignette, as the North Vietnamese 308th Division pressed its attack south, Lieutenant Colonel Turley ordered Captain Ripley and Major Smock to blow the bridge at Dong Ha. Captain Ripley determined that 500 pounds of explosives would have to be placed under the girders of the bridge. A chain link fence, topped with German steel tape, surrounded the base of the bridge. The two Americans quickly devised a plan. Captain Ripley would climb over the fence and emplace the explosives that Major Smock passed to him. Emplacing the explosives required Captain Ripley to hand-walk along the beams, exposing his dangling body to the enemy. For 2 hours, in the face of enemy small arms and tank fire, he set the charges. Finally, using the battery from a destroyed jeep, Captain Ripley detonated the charges, destroyed the bridge, and stopped the enemy armor in its tracks.[9] Captain Ripley's superb physical conditioning allowed him to pull off this amazing feat.

First Lieutenant Kenneth A. Conover, during 6 days of intense combat in Afghanistan, demonstrated the physical stamina required of leaders under stress.

> On 22 June 2012, First Lieutenant Conover led 1st Platoon, Company D, 1st Battalion, 7th Marines on a night air assault into the enemy stronghold of Qaleh Ye Gaz, Helmand Province, Afghanistan. As the platoon established its patrol base, the enemy attacked with medium machine gun fire, automatic rifle fire, and 10 rounds of 82-mm mortars. During the engagement, a mortar round landed 15 feet from First Lieutenant Conover. Luckily, the soft earth absorbed most of the blast. For the next 6 days, multiple waves of fanatical enemy fighters attacked the platoon. Within the first 2 days, First Lieutenant Conover led his platoon through the loss of two Marines, the serious wounding of another one, and the evacuation under fire of all three. He continued to lead his Marines through 23 direct fire engagements, 1 grenade attack, 2 indirect fire attacks, and 10 enemy attempts to overrun his position. In relentless pursuit of the enemy, he

> directed the employment of 38 tank main gun rounds, 4 artillery rocket strikes, 4 close air support strikes, 5 AT-4 rockets, and 2 anti-personnel obstacle breaching systems. His efforts resulted in clearing 2 square kilometers of enemy fighters and the capture of a high-value Taliban leader along with two other fighters.[10]

Not every Marine will face the same physical challenge as Captain Ripley nor will every Marine lead a platoon in combat like First Lieutenant Conover, but some will. Marine leaders understand this and work continuously to condition the Marines under their charge so that they overcome the physical challenges presented to them. A critical responsibility of every leader "is to ensure that members of his or her command have every survival

First Lieutenant Kenneth Conover on patrol in Afghanistan.

edge that can be provided. If people lack the coordinated response that comes only from long, varied and rigorous exercise, they will lack cohesion in action, have much higher combat losses and uselessly expend much of their initial velocity. . . . The gain in moral force deriving from all forms of physical training is an unconscious gain. Will power, determination, mental poise and muscle control all march hand in hand with the general health and well-being of the individual."[11]

Adaptability

Adaptability has long been our key to overcoming challenges. Although it is synonymous with flexibility, adaptability also embraces the spirit of innovation. Marines constantly seek to adapt new tactics, organization, and procedures to the realities of the environment. Marines identify deficiencies in existing practices, discard outdated structure, and make modifications to maintain function and utility. The ability to adapt enables Marines to be comfortable within an environment dominated by friction. Experience, common sense, and the critical application of judgment all help Marine leaders persevere.

Marines have long known how to adapt and overcome: 30 December 1927, a Marine patrol near Quilali, Nicaragua, engaged a large Sandinista force and suffered heavy casualties. The patrol was in desperate need of supplies and 18 Marines required medical evacuation. Marine pilots airdropped the equipment that was needed to

First Lieutenant Christian Schilt.

clear a 500-foot-long makeshift airstrip. Between 6 and 8 January 1928, First Lieutenant Christian F. Schilt risked his life to make 10 flights onto the airstrip in the besieged town carrying in a replacement commander and critical medical supplies. He also evacuated the 18 wounded Marines by strapping them to the wings in order to fly them out. His feat is even more incredible since the Vought O2U biplane had no brakes, which required Marines to arrest it by grabbing onto the wings and dragging the aircraft to a stop as soon as it touched down.[12]

Another example of innovation born out of the need to adapt was the use of Navajo Code Talkers. In the days before portable, tactical cryptographic devices, radio operators either had to transmit messages unencrypted risking enemy interception or laboriously encode, transmit, and decode messages. During World War I and after Pearl Harbor, the Army made limited use of Choctaw and Comanche speakers to transmit messages. Always on the lookout for innovative ideas, the Marine Corps followed the Army program with great interest. After a successful proof of concept, the Marine Corps enlisted 29 Navajo men for service as communicators. In keeping with Marine tradition, Commandant Thomas Holcomb insisted that the recruits receive the same basic training as other

Privates First Class Preston Toledo and Frank Toledo, Navajo Code Talkers, attached to a Marine artillery regiment in the South Pacific.

Marines. In other words, they were Marines first and specialists second. It turned out that the cryptographic solution was not as simple as speaking Navajo on the radio. The Navajo language didn't have an alphabet or words for military terms. The task of creating an alphabet and code words for military terminology fell on the new Marines. In the end, they created a code in their native language that reduced the time required to encode, transmit, and decode messages from 4 hours to about 2 minutes. As a result, the Navajo Code Talkers were combat multipliers in every campaign in the South Pacific, from Guadalcanal to Okinawa.[13]

Many years later, as Marine forces began to expand their lodgment during Operation Desert Shield, one of the greatest concerns was overland transportation. Faced with an acute shortage of trucks and other vehicles, Marine logisticians applied an unconventional approach to motor transportation. In addition to receiving 246 trucks from the Army, the Marines began leasing as many civilian vehicles as they could. In the end, they obtained 1,414 assorted trucks, which included 50 colorfully decorated 10-ton lorries that the Marines dubbed "circus trucks." Additionally, the Marines used 214 commercial buses and 465 sport utility vehicles to transport personnel.[14]

"Circus Truck" pressed into service during Operation Desert Storm.

Adaptation happens most frequently at the small unit level. During early August of 2010, Company L, 3d Battalion, 1st Marines attacked to clear the Taliban stronghold of Safar Bazaar in the Garmsir District of Helmand Province, Afghanistan. The Taliban who defended the bazaar saturated the area with IEDs. The lightweight, compact metal detector soon proved utterly useless against nonmetallic IEDs. Prior to the execution of the operation, the company came up with multiple nonstandard solutions to clearing the bazaar, one of which was water hoses. Safar Bazaar was conveniently located on a canal off the Helmand River so a nearly unlimited supply of water was available. The S-4 procured water pumps and hoses. It took 2 weeks to completely clear the bazaar using multiple kinetic and nonkinetic techniques, each complementing the other: line charges, Holley sticks (a field expedient stick and hook devised by Gunnery Sergeant Floyd Holley), and water hoses.

Although only 4 of the more than 100 IEDs discovered were found by using hoses during 3 months of operations in the Lima Company area of operations, it was 4 fewer devices that could have injured Marines or innocent civilians. The water also softened the soil, making it easier to dig into while they searched for pressure plates and wires.

Marines from Lima 3/1 clearing the Safar Bazaar.

INNOVATION

From the development of dive bombing in Nicaragua, to the pioneering of amphibious warfare between World Wars I and II, to operational maneuver from the sea, Marines have always sought innovative solutions to problems. Innovation requires that leaders listen to their subordinates.

Nowhere is our ability to innovate better demonstrated than in the development of our integrated air-ground combat team. The history of Marine aviation—since its inception in 1912—is a story of heroism, skill, and dedication and the continuous effort to develop better ways for air and ground forces to operate together. In aviation alone, Marines pioneered the development of close air support, helicopterborne operations, movable expeditionary airfields, dedicated airborne electronic warfare platforms, vertical/short takeoff and landing jets, expeditionary maintenance organizations and tilt-rotor assault support, and interoperable air command and control systems. Early attempts at close air support go back as far as 1919 when the first air units deployed to Haiti in support of ground forces. Beginning with pilots dropping small bombs out of open cockpits, aviators such as Lieutenant Lawson H.M. Sanderson began experimenting with dive bombing, which dramatically increased accuracy. The creation of the Fleet Marine Force in 1933 formalized the role of aviation as an element of the air-ground team. During the fleet landing exercises in the late 1930s, Marines developed the doctrine, techniques, and tactics that made close air support a reality in World War II.[15]

Our reputation as innovators stems, in part, from periodic examinations of our role in the national defense structure. After World War I, our predecessors sought to redefine the Corps, which had fought alongside the Army in the trenches in France. They focused on the requirement to seize advanced naval bases and developed doctrine for amphibious operations at a time when the other militaries of the world, in the aftermath of Gallipoli, considered it a reckless mission. By 1926, the Marine Corps was teaching courses in Pacific strategy and amphibious operations. It was in Marine Corps schools that students and faculty developed a list of chronological steps for planning and executing amphibious operations, resulting in the historic 1934 *Tentative Manual for Landing Operations*.[16] As Marines became experts in amphibious operations, they also trained US Army divisions in the tactics that would be used by them to land at Casablanca, Sicily, Anzio, and Normandy in the European theater; and at Kwajalein, Leyte, and Okinawa in the Pacific.[17] Marines went further still and developed a landing craft and a reef-crossing tractor that became primary tools in both the Pacific and European theaters of World War II.

During the landing exercises in 1924 in Culebra, Puerto Rico, Marines tested two types of landing craft: a 50-foot motor lighter based on the British "Beetle" boat and the Christie amphibian tank. Although the Marines successfully offloaded artillery from the "Beetle" boat, it still needed work. Though the Christie proved unseaworthy, it served as a forerunner to the amphibious tractor used during World War II. In the mid-1930s, the Marine Corps experimented with four modified commercial fishing boats and one metal surf boat. None of the five boats were found suitable due to problems that included exposed rudders and propellers that dug into the beach and a 10-foot drop for the Marines as they debarked. In 1938, the Navy tested the Eureka boat designed by Andrew Higgins. With a shallow draft and a tunnel to protect the propeller, the Eureka boat was able to land and then reverse off the beach. During exercises, the Marines had difficulty offloading personnel and equipment due to the high sides. After seeing a picture of a Japanese landing craft with a bow ramp conducting assault landing operations in Shanghai, Mr. Higgins added a ramp to his design, which led to the development of the [landing craft vehicle, personnel] LCVP.[18]

Higgins boat moves in to close in on smoke obscured island of Tarawa.

These innovations and others enabled the Marines to defeat the Japanese in a series of successful amphibious operations across the Pacific. After World War II, General Alexander A. Vandegrift summed up the importance of Marine Corps innovation during the interwar period, “Despite its outstanding record as a combat force in the past war, the Marine Corps’ far greater contribution to victory was doctrinal: that is, the fact that the basic amphibious doctrines which carried Allied troops over every beachhead of World War II had been largely shaped—often in the face of uninterested and doubting military orthodoxy—by U.S. Marines, and mainly between 1922 and 1935."[19] The Marine Corps also added to counterinsurgency doctrine by codifying its vast experience in operations other than war in the *Small Wars Manual* in 1940—a manual that continues to prove its relevance in the 21st century.

The innovations of Marine leaders have changed the character of war. Whether it was developing a system to use naval gunfire in support of landing forces, studying the art of dive bombing, figuring out how to drop bombs at night and in all kinds of weather, or developing and proving the concept of maritime prepositioning, they all demonstrated the impact of Marine leaders who combined vision and initiative.

Lieutenant General Victor A. Krulak developed a set of rules he followed to promote innovation and creativity. First, leaders should "make it [their] duty to bring [subordinates'] ideas and criticisms to the surface where all may analyze and evaluate them." Ask for ideas and you will get them. Second, leaders must "clear a path" to their doorstep. Subordinates should use the chain of command, but ideas must rise to the top. Leaders must allow subordinates the opportunity to show initiative. Third, because innovation is imprecise and because subordinates, especially junior ones, will make mistakes, protect them. "Zero defects" are not a standard of measurement. They do not encourage initiative; they stifle it. Lastly, emphasize that you expect honest expression of the subordinates' best thinking. Do not tolerate patronizing behavior![20]

Decentralization

Many years ago, there was a promotion examination question for lieutenants. The lieutenants were told that they had a 10-person working party, led by a sergeant, and must erect a 75-foot flagpole. Those lieutenants who tried to figure out how to erect the flagpole failed, no matter how accurate their calculations. The correct solution is to simply give the order, "Sergeant, put up that flagpole."[21] This question illustrates the point that decentralized leadership is taught, expected, and practiced throughout the Marine Corps. Decentralization is simply authorizing subordinates to act, guided by commander's intent and focus of effort, in situations where judgment and experience dictate action. The Marine Corps has long understood the advantage of allowing junior leaders to apply judgment and act on their decisions and has enjoyed great success decentralizing authority to the lowest levels. Marines fighting expeditionary wars during the first half of the 20th century exemplified this. Whether on duty in the Legation Quarter in China during the 1920's, with the *gendarmerie* in Haiti, or on patrol with the Guardia in Nicaragua, junior Marines—sergeants and lieutenants—supported United States policy; kept law and order; suppressed revolts against governments; and protected American lives, interests, and property.

During World War II, the actions of junior leaders were directly responsible for our successes in the island-hopping campaigns of the Pacific. Decentralized decisionmaking—pushing authority, responsibility, and accountability to the lowest levels—promoted speed in execution. In battle after battle, small units were able to make a decisive difference because of the actions of subordinate leaders. Of Tarawa, Colonel Merritt A. Edson mentioned decentralization and adaptability as important parts of the final outcome. "It is my opinion that the reason we won this show was the ability of the junior officers and noncoms to take command of small groups of six to eight or ten men, regardless of where these men came from, and to organize and lead them as a fighting team."[22]

As a result of these experiences, the Marine Corps developed the modern-day fire team and produced the world's finest noncommissioned officers. The tradition of encouraging decentralized decisionmaking continues today and is manifested in such peacetime duty as that performed by Marine Security Guard detachments commanded by staff noncommissioned officers, drill instructors at recruit depots and Officer Candidates School, and the small-unit combat patrols in the strife-torn streets of every corner of the globe.

Testimony to the skills of Marine small-unit leaders was the development of the combined action program. First used with success in Haiti (1915–1934), then later in Santo Domingo (1916–1922) and Nicaragua (1926–1933), and then used again in Vietnam.[23] Often, the combined force was commanded by a Marine squad leader—a sergeant or a corporal. In Iraq and Afghanistan, this concept took the form of small training and advising teams embedding with Iraqi and Afghan security forces.

Marine advisor in Afghanistan.

THE INDOMITABLE WILL TO WIN

A great and successful troop leader said that there comes a point in every close battle when each commander concludes that he is defeated. The leader who carries on, wins.

Positions are seldom lost because they have been destroyed, but almost invariably because the leader has decided in his own mind that the position cannot be held.[24]

—Items 36 and 38 from *Battle Doctrine for Front Line Leaders*

All leaders lead in much the same way. Why then, do some Marine leaders succeed and others fail? What is it that some leaders have that others do not? The common trait of successful leaders is an indomitable will to win that enables them to face the most challenging of tasks and extract the most from their subordinates.

> Captain William Barber's Medal of Honor citation reflects how his performance from 28 November 1950 to 2 December 1950 demonstrates the importance of a leader's will. Captain Barber received the mission to defend a critical 3-mile long mountain pass along the 1st Marine Division's main supply route. Captain Barber's battle weary Marines dug in positions in the frozen, snow-covered hillside. That night, an estimated regimental strength force savagely attacked over a 7-hour period, inflicting heavy casualties. After repulsing the enemy, Captain Barber assured his higher headquarters that he could hold his isolated position if supplied by air drops. He understood that if he abandoned his defensive position, 8,000 Marines would be trapped at Yudam-ni and would not be able to join the 3,000 more awaiting their arrival at Hagaru-ri for the continued drive to the sea. Despite severe wounds that forced him to be carried on a litter, Captain Barber continued to lead his Marines. Through 5 days and 6 nights of repeated attacks by the Chinese, he and his courageous Marines held, killing approximately 1,000 enemy combatants in the bitter subzero weather. When the company was finally relieved, only 82 of his original 220 men were able to walk off the hill under their own power. Captain Barber's indomitable will inspired his men and allowed the 1st Marine Division to avoid destruction by withdrawing from the Chosin Reservoir.[25]

It is tough-minded leaders like Captain Barber that hold units together under extreme stress. Lieutenant Colonel Murray, commanding the 5th Marines at the Chosin Reservoir, summed up what was required of leaders: "I personally felt in a state of shock, the kind of shock one gets from some great personal tragedy, the sudden loss of someone close. . . . My first fight was within myself. I had to rebuild that emptiness of spirit."[26] For leaders to hold units together under adverse conditions, they must first fight—and win—the battle within themselves.

Combat Power and Winning

Combat power is "the total means of destructive and/or disruptive force which a military unit/formation can apply against the opponent at a given time."[27] Napoleon clearly understood that the combat power of a unit is not measured solely by the number of people, rifles, tanks, cannons, trucks, fuel, ammunition, or airplanes a military force possesses when he said, "The moral is to the physical as three to one."[28] By moral, Napoleon meant those mental and spiritual qualities of a unit. The moral quality is an organization's ability to conduct combat operations by overcoming challenges faced on the battlefield. Creating and sustaining superior combat power requires the combination of the tangible activities of war—maneuver, firepower, and protection—with the intangible elements of war—unit *esprit*, discipline, cohesion, and individual courage. It is these intangible qualities that make certain units superior to others on the battlefield. They enable organizations to take high casualties and continue their missions and can compensate for material deficiencies. It is the leaders who instill these intangible qualities in their Marines. In the end, "***Success in battle is not a function of how many show up, but who they are.***"[29]

This Page Intentionally Left Blank

Epilogue

General Carl E. Mundy, Jr.

Because of engaged, compassionate, and caring leaders, serving in the Marine Corps is a defining experience for everyone who has worn our cloth. Generations of Marines accepted this sacred responsibility. This challenge is now passed to you. Thus it is fitting to end this version of *Leading Marines* with the words of General Mundy, its original author.

"The most important responsibility in our Corps is leading Marines. If we expect Marines to lead and if we expect Marines to follow, we must provide the education of the heart and of the mind to win on the battlefield and in the barracks, in war and in peace. Traditionally, that education has taken many forms, often handed down from Marine to Marine, by word of mouth and by example.

"Our actions as Marines every day must embody the legacy of those who went before us. Their memorial to us—their teaching, compassion, courage, sacrifices, optimism, humor, humility, commitment, perseverance, love, guts, and glory—is the pattern for our daily lives. This manual attempts to capture those heritages of the Marine Corps' approach to leading. It is not prescriptive because there is no formula for leadership. It is not all-inclusive because to capture all that it is to be a Marine or to lead Marines defies pen and paper. Instead, it is intended to provide those charged with leading Marines a sense of the legacy they have inherited, and to help them come to terms with their own personal leadership style. The indispensable condition of Marine Corps leadership is action and attitude, not words. As one Marine leader said, 'Don't tell me how good you are. Show me!'

"Marines have been leading for over 200 years and today continue leading around the globe. Whether in the field or in garrison, at the front or in the rear, Marines, adapting the time-honored values, traditions, customs, and history of our Corps to their generation, will continue to lead—and continue to win.

"This manual comes to life through the voices, writings, and examples of not one person, but many. Thousands of Americans who have borne, and still bear, the title 'Marine' are testimony that 'Once a Marine, Always a Marine' and '*Semper Fidelis*' are phrases that define our essence. It is to those who know, and to those who will come to know, this extraordinary way of life that this book is dedicated."

Semper Fidelis . . .

Appendices

The appendices contain several foundational documents that guide leaders of Marines. Just like the rest of *Leading Marines*, these documents are not meant to be read passively nor are they meant to sit on a book shelf or decorate an "I-love-me-wall." It is the responsibility of all Marine leaders to read and understand these documents and to discuss them not only with their subordinates but also amongst themselves.

The Oaths

Every young man and woman entering the Armed Forces takes an oath to "support and defend the Constitution of the United States"—it is the Constitution that represents the ideas and ideals on which the United States was formed. In taking this sacred oath, Marines pledge their lives to honorably, faithfully, and loyally serve the Nation, which is part of what makes military service a profession.

Marine Corps Manual, Paragraph 1100

Paragraph 1100, "Military Leadership," from the *Marine Corps Manual* describes what is expected of Marine noncommissioned, staff noncommissioned, and commissioned officers and the associated special trust and confidence reposed in them.

Promotion Warrants and Commissions

Each enlisted warrant and officer commission begins by "reposing special trust and confidence" in the promotee. Once granted, it is the Marine's responsibility to maintain this special trust and confidence by adhering to our core values. These documents also define the basic authority to issue orders to those of lesser rank and the responsibility to carefully and diligently discharge his or her duties.

The Creeds

The Noncommissioned Officer Creed and Staff Noncommissioned Officer Creed outline the expectations and ideals that guide the conduct of Marine leaders. As the embodiment of professional conduct, uncompromising discipline, and technical proficiency, the contributions of the noncommissioned and staff noncommissioned officers are vital to the effectiveness and efficiency of the command. These creeds reaffirm the obligations and responsibilities that these leaders have to their Marines, as well as their commander.

This Page Intentionally Left Blank

The Oaths

The following oaths are taken from: United States Code, Title 10, *Armed Forces*, subtitle A, part II, chap. 31, sec. 502, Enlistment Oath, and MCO P1400.31_, *Marine Corps Promotion Manual, Volume 1, Officer Promotions*, para 6006.2.

Oath of Enlistment

I, ______________, do solemnly swear (or affirm) that I will support and defend the Constitution of the United States against all enemies, foreign and domestic; that I will bear true faith and allegiance to the same; and that I will obey the orders of the President of the United States and the orders of the officers appointed over me, according to regulations and the Uniform Code of Military Justice. So help me God.

Commissioning Oath

I, ______________, do solemnly swear (or affirm) that I will support and defend the Constitution of the United States against all enemies, foreign and domestic; that I will bear true faith and allegiance to the same; that I take this obligation freely, without any mental reservation or purpose of evasion; and that I will well and faithfully discharge the duties of the office on which I am about to enter. So help me God.

This Page Intentionally Left Blank

Marine Corps Manual, Paragraph 1100

The following excerpt is from the *Marine Corps Manual*, with Changes 1–3 incorporated.

SECTION B—MANAGEMENT

1100. MILITARY LEADERSHIP

1. Purpose and Scope

a. The objective of Marine Corps Leadership is to develop the leadership qualities of Marines to enable them to assume progressively greater responsibilities to the Marine Corps and society.

b. Marine Corps Leadership qualities include:

(1) Inspiration—Personal example of high moral standards reflecting virtue, honor, patriotism, and subordination in personal behavior and in performance.

(2) Technical proficiency—Knowledge of the military sciences and skill in their application.

(3) Moral responsibility—Personal adherence to high standards of conduct and the guidance of subordinates toward wholesomeness of mind and body.

2. Responsibility

a. The Commandant of the Marine Corps is directly responsible to the Secretary of the Navy for establishing and maintaining leadership standards and conducting leadership training within the Marine Corps.

b. Commanders will ensure that local policies, directives and procedures reflect the special trust and confidence reposed in members of the officer corps. Full credit will be given to their statements and certificates. They will be allowed maximum discretion in the exercise of authority vested in them, and they and their dependents will be accorded all prerogatives and perquisites which are traditional and otherwise appropriate. Except in cases where more stringent positive identification procedures are required for the proper security of classified material and installations, or are imposed by higher authority for protecting privileges reserved for eligible military personnel, the officers' uniforms will amply attest to their status, and their oral statements will serve to identify them and their dependents.

c. An individual's responsibility for leadership is not dependent upon authority. Marines are expected to exert proper influence upon their comrades by setting examples of obedience, courage, zeal, sobriety, neatness, and attention to duty.

d. The special trust and confidence, which is expressly reposed in officers by their commission, is the distinguishing privilege of the officer corps. It is the policy of the Marine Corps that this privilege be tangible and real; it is the corresponding obligation of the officer corps that it be wholly deserved.

(1) As an accompanying condition commanders will impress upon all subordinate officers the fact that the presumption of integrity, good manners, sound judgment, and discretion, which is the basis for the special trust and confidence reposed in each officer, is jeopardized by the slightest transgression on the part of any member of the officer corps. Any offense, however minor, will be dealt with promptly, and with sufficient severity to impress on the officer at fault, and on the officer corps. Dedication to the basic elements of special trust and confidence is a Marine officer's obligation to the officer corps as a whole, and transcends the bonds of personal friendship.

(2) As a further and continuing action, commanders are requested to bring to the attention of higher authority, referencing this paragraph, any situation, policy, directive, or procedure which contravenes the spirit of this paragraph, and which is not susceptible to local correction.

(3) Although this policy is expressly concerned with commissioned officers, its provisions and spirit will, where applicable, be extended to noncommissioned officers, especially staff noncommissioned officers.

3. Personal Relations. Effective personal relations in an organization can be satisfactory only when there is complete understanding and respect between individuals. Commanders must:

a. Strive for forceful and competent leadership throughout the entire organization.

b. Inform the troops of plans of action and reasons therefor, whenever it is possible and practicable to do so.

c. Endeavor to remove on all occasions those causes which make [f]or misunderstanding or dissatisfaction.

d. Assure that all members of the command are acquainted with procedures for registering complaints, together with the action taken thereon.

e. Build a feeling of confidence which will ensure the free approach by subordinates for advice and assistance not only in military matters but for personal problems as well.

4. Professional and personal relationships between Marines. Professional and personal relationships, including duty, social, and business contacts among Marines of different grades will be consistent with traditional standards of good order and discipline and the mutual [r]espect that has always existed between Marines of senior grade and those of lesser grade. Personal relationships between officer and enlisted members that are unduly familiar and that do not respect differences in grade or rank constitute **fraternization** and are prohibited. When prejudicial to good order and discipline or of a nature to bring discredit on the Marine Corps, personal relationships between officer members or between enlisted members that are unduly familiar and that do not respect differences in grade or rank constitute **fraternization** and are prohibited. Prejudice to good order and discipline or discredit to the Marine Corps may result from any circumstance which calls into question a senior's objectivity, results in actual or apparent preferential treatment, undermines the authority of the senior, or compromises the chain of command. The following paragraphs written by Major General John A. Lejeune appeared in the Marine Corps Manual, edition of 1921, and since that time have defined the relationship that must exist between Marine officers and enlisted

members, as well as between officers of different grades and enlisted members of different grades of the Corps and other military Service members.

a."Comradeship and brotherhood.—The World War wrought a great change in the relations between officers and enlisted men in the military services. A spirit of comradeship and brotherhood in arms came into being in the training camps and on the battlefields. This spirit is too fine a thing to be allowed to die. It must be fostered and kept alive and made the moving force in all Marine Corps organizations."

b. "Teacher and scholar.—The relation between officers and enlisted men should in no sense be that of superior and inferior nor that of master and servant, but rather that of teacher and scholar. In fact, it should partake of the nature of the relation between father and son, to the extent that officers, especially commanding officers, are responsible for the physical, mental, and moral welfare, as well as the discipline and military training of the young men under their command who are serving the nation in the Marine Corps."

c. "The realization of this responsibility on the part of officers is vital to the well-being of the Marine Corps. It is especially so, for the reason that so large a proportion of the men enlisting are under twenty-one years of age. These men are in the formative period of their lives, and officers owe it to them, to their parents, and to the nation, that when discharged from the services they should be far better men physically, mentally, and morally than they were when they enlisted."

d. "To accomplish this task successfully a constant effort must be made by all officers to fill each day with useful and interesting instruction and wholesome entertainment for the men. This effort must be intelligent and not perfunctory, the object being not only to do away with idleness, but to train and cultivate the bodies, the minds, and the spirit of our men."

e. "Love of corps and country.—To be more specific, it will be necessary for officers not only to devote their close attention to the many questions affecting the comfort, health, military training and discipline of the men under their command, but also actively to promote athletics and to endeavor to enlist the interest of their men in building up and maintaining their bodies in the finest physical condition; to encourage them to enroll in the Marine Corps Institute and to keep up their studies after enrollment; and to make every effort by means of historical, educational and patriotic address to cultivate in their hearts a deep abiding love of the corps and country."

f. "Leadership.—Finally, it must be kept in mind that the American soldier responds quickly and readily to the exhibition of qualities of leadership on the part of his officers. Some of these qualities are industry, energy, initiative, determination, enthusiasm, firmness, kindness, justness, self-control, unselfishness, honor, and courage. Every officer should endeavor by all means in his power to make himself the possessor of these qualities and thereby to fit himself to be a real leader of men."

5. Noncommissioned officers. The provisions of paragraphs 1100.3 and 1100.4 above, apply to the relationship of noncommissioned officers with their subordinates and apply specifically

to noncommissioned officers who may be exercising supervisory authority or leadership roles over junior Marines.

6. Officer and enlisted marriages. The Marine Corps accepts officer/enlisted marriages which occur before the officer receives a commission or before the officer reverts to an enlisted grade. However, misconduct, including fraternization, is neither excused nor mitigated by subsequent marriage between the parties. Marines married to other Marines or to other Service members, or otherwise closely related (e.g., parent/child, siblings) shall maintain the requisite traditional respect and decorum attending the official military relationship between them while either is on duty, in uniform in public, or at official social functions.

This Page Intentionally Left Blank

Promotion Warrants and Commissions

JUNIOR ENLISTED
PROMOTION WARRANT

To all who shall see these presents, greeting:

Know Ye, that reposing special trust and confidence in the fidelity and abilities of ____, I do appoint this Marine a ________________________________ in the

United States Marine Corps

to rank as such from the __________ day of ________________, two thousand _________________.

This appointee will therefore carefully and diligently discharge the duties of the grade to which appointed by doing and performing all manner of things thereunto pertaining. And I do strictly charge and require all personnel of lesser grade to render obedience to appropriate orders. And this appointee is to observe and follow such orders and directions as may be given from time to time by Superiors acting according to the rules and articles governing the discipline of the ***Armed Forces of the United States of America.***

Given under my hand at _____________________________________
this __________ day of _____________________, in the year of our Lord two thousand ________________.

NONCOMMISSIONED OFFICERS
PROMOTION WARRANT

To all who shall see these presents, greetings:

Know Ye, that reposing special trust and confidence in the fidelity and abilities of ____, I do appoint this Marine a ____ in the

United States Marine Corps

to rank as such from the _______ day of ____________, two thousand ______ .

"Effective with this appointment, you are charged to carefully and diligently execute the duties and responsibilities of a _______________ of Marines, and I do strictly direct and require all personnel of lesser grade to render obedience to appropriate orders. As a _______________ of Marines you must set the example for others to emulate. Your conduct and professionalism both on and off duty shall be above reproach. You are responsible for the accomplishment of your assigned mission and for the safety, professional development and well-being of the Marines in your charge. You will be the embodiment of our institutional core values of honor, courage and commitment. You will lead your Marines with firmness, fairness and dignity while observing and following the orders and directions of your senior leaders and enforcing all regulations and articles governing the discipline of the ***Armed Forces of the United States of America."***

Given under my hand at ____

this __________ day of _________________________, in the year of our Lord two thousand ________________.

STAFF NONCOMMISSIONED OFFICERS
PROMOTION WARRANT

To all who shall see these presents, greetings:

Know Ye, that reposing special trust and confidence in the fidelity and abilities of ____, I do appoint this Marine a ____________________________________ in the

United States Marine Corps

to rank as such from the ________ day of ____________________, two thousand _____________.

This appointee will therefore carefully and diligently discharge the duties of the grade to which appointed by doing and performing all manner of things thereunto pertaining. And I do strictly charge and require all personnel of lesser grade to render obedience to appropriate orders. And this appointee is to observe and follow such orders and directions as may be given from time to time by Superiors acting according to the rules and articles governing the discipline of the ***Armed Forces of the United States of America.***

Given under my hand at ***Headquarters United States Marine Corps*** *this ____________ day of _______________________, in the year of our Lord two thousand _________________.*

WARRANT OFFICER
PROMOTION WARRANT

To all who shall see these presents, greeting:

Know Ye, that reposing special trust and confidence in the patriotism, valor, fidelity and abilities of ____ I do appoint ____ in the

United States Marine Corps

to rank as such from the ________ day of __________________________ two thousand _____________. This Officer will therefore carefully and diligently discharge the duties of the grade to which appointed by doing and performing all manner of things thereunto belonging.

And I do strictly charge and require those Officers and other personnel of lesser rank to render such obedience as is due an officer of this grade and position. And this Officer is to observe and follow orders and directions, from time to time, as may be given by me, or other Superior Officers acting in accordance with the laws of the United States of America.

This warrant is to continue in force during the pleasure of the Secretary of the Navy, for the time being, under the provisions of those Public Laws relating to Officers of the ***Armed Forces of the United States of America*** *and the component thereof in which this appointment is made.*

Done at the City of Washington, this __________ day of _________________ in the year of our Lord two thousand ____________________________________ and of the Independence of the United States of America the two hundred ______.

COMPANY GRADE OFFICER COMMISSION

To all who shall see these presents, greeting:

Know ye that, reposing special trust and confidence in the patriotism, valor, fidelity and abilities of ______________________________ I do appoint this officer a ________________________ in the

United States Marine Corps

To rank as such from the ____ day of _________ two thousand ___. This officer will therefore carefully and diligently discharge the duties of the office to which appointed by doing and performing all manner of things thereunto belonging.

And I do strictly charge and require those officers and other personnel of lesser rank to render such obedience as is due an officer of this grade and position. And this officer is to observe and follow orders and directions, from time to time, as may be given by the President of the United States of America, or other superior officers acting in accordance with the laws of the United States of America.

This commission is to continue in force during the pleasure of the President of the United States of America under the provisions of those public laws relating to officers of the ***Armed Forces of the United States of America*** *and the component thereof in which this appointment is made.*

Done at the City of Washington, this ____ day of __________ in the year of our Lord ________ and of the Independence of the United States of America, the two hundred _______________.

A-19

FIELD GRADE OFFICER COMMISSION

To all who shall see these presents, greeting:

Know ye that, reposing special trust and confidence in the patriotism, valor, fidelity and ability of ____ I do by and with the consent of the Senate, appoint this officer

____ in the

United States Marine Corps

To rank as such from the ____ day of _________ two thousand ___. This officer will therefore carefully and diligently discharge the duties of the office to which appointed by doing and performing all manner of things thereunto belonging.

And I do strictly charge and require those officers and other personnel of lesser rank to render such obedience as is due an officer of this grade and position. And this officer is to observe and follow orders and directions, from time to time, as may be given by the President of the United States of America, or other superior officers acting in accordance with the laws of the United States of America.

This commission is to continue in force during the pleasure of the President of the United States of America under the provisions of those public laws relating to officers of the ***Armed Forces of the United States of America*** *and the component thereof in which this appointment is made.*

Done at the city of Washington, this ____ day of __________ in the year of our Lord ________ and the Independence of the United States of America, the two hundred _______________.

The Creeds

The Noncommissioned Officers Creed is taken from NAVMC Directive 1500.58, *Marine Corps Mentoring Program Guidebook*, appendix 106. The Staff Noncommissioned Officers Creed is taken from NAVMC Directive 1500.58, *Marine Corps Mentoring Program Guidebook*, appendix 106.

NCO Creed

I am the backbone of the United States Marine Corps, I am a Marine Noncommissioned Officer. I serve as part of the vital link between my commander (and all officers) and enlisted Marines. I will never forget who I am or what I represent. I will challenge myself to the limit and be ever attentive to duty. I am now, more than ever, committed to excellence in all that I do, so that I can set the proper example for other Marines. I will demand of myself all the energy, knowledge and skills I possess, so that I can instill confidence in those I teach. I will constantly strive to perfect my own skills and to become a good leader. Above all I will be truthful in all I say or do. My integrity shall be impeccable as my appearance. I will be honest with myself, with those under my charge and with my superiors. I pledge to do my best to incorporate all the leadership traits into my character. For such is the heritage I have received from that long, illustrious line of professionals who have worn the bloodstripe so proudly before me. I must give the very best I have for my Marines, my Corps and my Country for though today I instruct and supervise in peace, tomorrow, I may lead in war.

Staff NCO Creed

I am a Staff Noncommissioned Officer in the United States Marine Corps. As such, I am a member of the most unique group of professional military practitioners in the world. I am bound by duty to God, Country and my fellow Marines to execute the demands of my position to and beyond what I believe to be the limits of my capabilities.

I realize I am the mainstay of Marine Corps discipline, and I carry myself with military grace, unbowed by the weight of command, unflinching in the execution of lawful orders, and unwavering in my dedication to the most complete success of my assigned mission.

Both my professional and personal demeanor shall be such that I may take pride if my juniors emulate me, and knowing perfection to lie beyond the grasp of any mortal hand, I shall yet strive to attain perfection that I may ever be aware of my needs and capabilities to improve myself. I shall be fair in my personal relations, just in the enforcement of discipline, true to myself and my fellow Marines, and equitable in my dealing with everyone.

Notes

Chapter 1—Our Ethos

1. *Journal of the Continental Congress*, 10 November 1775, in *Naval Documents of the American Revolution*, Vol. 2, ed. William Bell Clark (Washington, D.C.: Government Printing Office, 1966) p. 972.

2. Lieutenant General Victor H. Krulak, USMC (Ret.), *First To Fight: An Inside View of the U.S. Marine Corps* (Annapolis, MD: Naval Institute Press, 1984) p. 155.

3. Ibid, p. 155.

4. This quote is used with permission from Glenn B. Knight owner and moderator of the myMarine Group and editor of the "Marine Quotes" website: <http://oldcorps.org/USMC/quotes.html> (accessed: 7 January 2014).

5. FMFRP 12-46, *Advanced Base Operations in Micronesia* (August 1992), p. 41. FMFRP 12-46 is a historical reprint of Operation Plan 712 written by Major Earl H. Ellis in 1921.

6. Clark, p. 972.

7. Paraphrased from US House of Representatives, 82nd Congress, 1st Session, Report No. 666 from the Committee on Armed Services, 30 June 1951, p. 6, <http://hdl.handle.net/2027/mdp.35112102288109> (accessed: 11 June 2014).

8. Richard Rubin, *The Last of the Doughboys: The Forgotten Generation and Their Forgotten World War* (Boston: Houghton Mifflin Harcourt, 2013) p. 192.

9. Captain Henry T. Elrod on *navy.mil*. <http://www.elrod.navy.mil> (accessed: 21 February 2014).

10. Paraphrased from NAVMC 11533 (EF), *Personal Award Recommendation*, Summary of Action and Award Citation for Lieutenant Colonel Christopher K. Raible's actions on 14 September 2012 during Operation Enduring Freedom. Lieutenant Colonel Raible was awarded the Bronze Star with Combat "V."

11. Paraphrased from NAVMC 11533 (EF), *Personal Award Recommendation*, Summary of Action and Award Citation for Sergeant Bradley W. Atwell's actions from 19 April to 14 September 2012 during Operation Enduring Freedom. Sergeant Atwell was awarded the Navy and Marine Corps Commendation Medal with Combat "V."

12. Paraphrased from NAVMC 11533 (EF), *Personal Award Recommendation*, Summary of Action and Award Citation for Major Robb T. McDonald's actions on 14 September 2012 during Operation Enduring Freedom. Major McDonald was awarded the Silver Star.

13. William Manchester, *Goodbye, Darkness: A Memoir of the Pacific War* (Boston: Little, Brown and Company, 1980) p. 391.

14. Andrew Geer, *The New Breed: The Story of the U.S. Marines in Korea* (Nashville, TN: The Battery Press, 1989) pp. 281–282.

15. Paraphrased from NAVMC 11533 (EF), *Personal Award Recommendation,* Summary of Action and Award Citation for First Sergeant Bradley A. Kasal's actions on 13 November 2004 during Operation Iraqi Freedom. First Sergeant Kasal was awarded the Navy Cross.

16. Captain John W. Thomason, Jr., USMC, *Fix Bayonets!* (New York: Charles Scribner's Sons, 1927) p. xiv.

17. On 25 October 1983, 2 days after the bombing, then Commandant of the Marine Corps, General P. X. Kelley, visited the US Air Force Regional Medical Center in Wiesbaden, Germany, where he met with Lance Corporal Jeffrey Nashton who had been critically injured.

18. Marine Corps Historical Reference Series, No. 22, *Marine Corps Lore* (Washington, D.C.: Headquarters, US Marine Corps, G-3 Division, Historical Branch, 1960) pp. 2, 8-9, and 11.

19. Armed Forces Information Service, *The Armed Forces Officer* (Washington, D.C.: Department of Defense, 1975) pp. 56–57.

20. A letter to General L. F. Chapman, Jr., USMC, as cited in a letter to All General Officers and All Commanding Officers, dated 19 July 1971, with minor textual changes.

Chapter 2—Foundations of Leadership

1. MCDP 1, *Warfighting* (Washington, D.C.: Headquarters, US Marine Corps, 1997) p. 57.

2. MCO 29, *Relations between Officers and Men* (Washington, D.C.: Headquarters, US Marine Corps, 1920).

3. Ibid.

4. Major General John A. Lejeune, "A Legacy of Esprit and Leadership," (speech presented to Army General Staff College [forerunner of the Army War College] in Washington, D.C., 18 January 1921), as reprinted in *Marine Corps Gazette* (July 1979) p. 32.

5. Lieutenant Colonel Dave Grossman, *On Killing: The Psychological Cost of Learning to Kill in War and Society* (New York: Back Bay Books; Little, Brown and Company, 1996) p. 85.

6. Lejeune, "A Legacy of Esprit and Leadership," p. 31.

7. Paraphrased from the Presidential Unit Citation as quoted in Jane Blakeney, *Heroes: U.S. Marine Corps 1861–1953—Armed Forces Awards-Flags*, "First Marine Division, Reinforced" (Washington, D.C.: Guthrie Lithograph Co., 1957) p. 362. The 1st Marine Division, Reinforced, received the Presidential Unit Citation for actions in Chosin Reservoir and the Koto-ri area of Korea from 27 November to 11 December 1950.

8. Allan R. Millett, *Semper Fidelis: The Story of the United States Marine Corps* (New York: Macmillan Publishing Co., 1980) p. 498.

9. Major Ted McKeldin, USMCR, *From the Horse's Mouth: Selected Thoughts on Small-Unit Leadership*, 2nd ed. (Quantico, VA: Marine Corps Association, 2004) p. 9.

10. Ibid, p. 8.

11. Colonel B. P. McCoy, *The Passion of Command: The Moral Imperative of Leadership* (Quantico, VA: Marine Corps Association, 2007) p. 37.

12. Corporal Gary C. Cooper, "Guideposts to Leadership," *Marine Corps Gazette* (July 1960) p. 35.

13. A letter to the officers of the Marine Corps from Major General Lejeune.

14. *Marine Corps Manual* (w/changes 1–3), Paragraph 1100.1b(1), (Washington, D.C.: Headquarters, US Marine Corps, 21 March 1980) p. 1-21.

15. Major General John A. Lejeune, USMC, *The Reminiscences of a Marine* (Quantico, VA: Marine Corps Association, 1990) p. 100.

16. Paraphrased from the Medal of Honor citation presented to First Lieutenant William D. Hawkins as quoted in *The Congressional Medal of Honor: The Names, The Deeds* (Forest Ranch, CA: Sharp and Dunnigan Publications, 1984) pp. 341–42.

17. From CMC correspondence files.

18. Paraphrased from the Navy Cross citation presented to Corporal James J. Barrett as quoted in *The Navy Cross: Vietnam*, ed. Paul D. Stevens (Forest Ranch, CA: Sharp and Dunnigan Publications, 1987) p. 25.

19. Paraphrased from NAVMC 11533 (EF), *Personal Award Recommendation*, Summaries of Action and Award Citations for Corporal Dakota L. Meyer and Staff Sergeant Juan J. Rodriguez-Chavez for their actions on 8 September 2009 during Operation Enduring Freedom. Corporal Meyer was awarded the Medal of Honor and Staff Sergeant Rodriguez-Chavez was awarded the Navy Cross.

20. MCDP 1, *Warfighting*, pp. 14–15.

21. Adapted from Charles Edmundson, "Why Warriors Fight," *Marine Corps Gazette* (September 1944) p. 3.

22. Paraphrased from NAVMC 11533 (EF), *Personal Award Recommendation*, Summary of Action and Award Citation for Corporal Jason L. Dunham's actions on 14 April 2004 during Operation Iraqi Freedom. Corporal Dunham was awarded the Medal of Honor posthumously.

23. Paraphrased from NAVMC 11533 (EF), *Personal Award Recommendation*, Summary of Action and Award Citation for Lance Corporal William K. Carpenter's actions on 21 November 2010 during Operation Enduring Freedom. Lance Corporal Carpenter was awarded the Medal of Honor.

24. Colonel Mary Stremlowe, USMCR, *A History of Women Marines 1946–1977* (Washington, D.C.: Headquarters, US Marine Corps, History and Museums Division, 1986) pp. 169–170.

25. Edmundson, "Why Warriors Fight," p. 8.

Chapter 3—Overcoming Challenges

1. Carl von Clausewitz, *On War*, trans. and ed. by Michael Howard and Peter Paret, (Princeton, NJ: Princeton University Press, 1989) pp. 187–188. This unfinished classic is arguably the definitive treatment of the nature and theory of war. All Marine officers should consider this book essential reading.

2. Ibid., p. 119.

3. MCRP 6-11B, *Marine Corps Values: A User's Guide for Discussion Leaders*, "Combat Leadership," (Washington, D.C.: Headquarters, US Marine Corps, 1998) p. 21–11.

4. At the time of the *Mayaguez* incident, the billet title "Commander in Chief Pacific Command (CINCPAC)" was the correct title for this billet. However, per the Secretary of Defense memo, dated 24 October 2002, the title of "Commander in Chief" belongs only to the President of the United States and not to military commanders.

5. Major George R. Dunham, USMC, and Colonel David A. Quinlan, USMC, *U.S. Marines in Vietnam: The War That Would Not End* 1973–1975 (Washington, D.C.: Headquarters, US Marine Corps, History and Museums Division,1990) pp. 238–265.

6. Lejeune, *The Reminiscences of a Marine*, pp. 414–415.

7. Major Charles D. Melson, USMC, and Lieutenant Colonel Curtis G. Arnold, USMC, *U.S. Marines in Vietnam: The War That Would Not End 1971–1973* (Washington, D.C.: History and Museums Division, Headquarters, US Marine Corps, 1991) pp. 50–56.

8. As quoted in *Respectfully Quoted: A Dictionary of Quotations Requested from the Congressional Research Service,* ed. Suzy Platt (Washington, D.C.: Library of Congress, 1989) entry 1635.

9. Colonel Gerald H. Turley, USMCR, (Ret.), *The Easter Offensive: The Last American Advisors Vietnam, 1972* (Novato, CA: Presidio Press, 1985) pp. 155–162.

10. Paraphrased from NAVMC 11533 (EF), *Personal Award Recommendation,* Summary of Action for First Lieutenant Kenneth A. Conover's actions from 22 to 27 June 2012 during Operation Enduring Freedom. First Lieutenant Conover was awarded the Silver Star.

11. Armed Forces Information Service, *The Armed Forces Officer* (Washington, D.C.: Department of Defense, 1975) pp. 62–63.

12. Lieutenant Colonel Edward C. Johnson, USMC, *Marine Corps Aviation: The Early Years 1912—1940*, ed. by Graham A. Cosmas (Washington, D.C.: Headquarters, US Marine Corps, History and Museums Division, 1991) p. 57.

13. Sally McClain, *Navajo Weapon: The Navajo Code Talkers* (Tucson, AZ: Rio Nuevo Publishers, 2001) pp. 21, 23, 34, 52, 54, 55, 67, 68, and 220.

14. Charles J. Quilter, *U.S. Marines in the Persian Gulf, 1990–1991: With the I Marine Expeditionary Force in Desert Shield and Desert Storm* (Washington, D.C.: Headquarters, US Marine Corps, History and Museums Division, 1993) pp. 28–29.

15. Johnson, pp. *v*, 49, and 53.

16. Lieutenant Colonel Kenneth J. Clifford, USMCR, *Progress and Purpose: A Developmental History of the United States Marine Corps 1900–1970* (Washington, D.C.: Headquarters, US Marine Corps, History and Museums Division, 1973) pp. 37–38 and 46.

17. J. Robert Moskin, *The U.S. Marine Corps Story*, 3rd rev. ed. (Boston: Little, Brown and Company, 1992) p. 225.

18. Clifford, pp. 33–35 and 49–57.

19. Moskin, p. 224.

20. Lieutenant General Victor A. Krulak, USMC (Ret.), "A Soldier's Dilemma," *Marine Corps Gazette* (November 1986) pp. 29–31.

21. Colonel Robert D. Heinl, Jr., USMC (Ret.), *The Marine Officer's Guide*, 4th ed. (Annapolis, MD: Naval Institute Press, 1977) p. 374.

22. Jon T. Hoffman, *Once A Legend: "Red Mike" Edson of the Marine Raiders* (Novato, CA: Presidio Press, 1994) p. 249.

23. Krulak, *First to Fight*, p. 190.

24. *Battle Doctrine For Front Line Leaders* (Quantico, VA: Marine Corps Development and Education Command, US Marine Corps Education Center, 1981) p. 7. This publication was originally written and published as a training guide by the 3d Marine Division, Fleet Marine Force, under the command of General A. A. Vandegrift during World War II.

25. Paraphrased from the Medal of Honor citation presented to Captain William E. Barber as quoted in *The Congressional Medal of Honor: The Names, The Deeds* (Forest Ranch, CA: Sharp and Dunnigan Publications, 1984) pp. 35–36.

26. T. R. Fehrenbach, *This Kind of War: The Classic Korean War History* (Washington: Brassey's, 1994) p. 246.

27. JP 1-02, *Department of Defense Dictionary of Military and Associated Terms*, 8 November 2010 (As Amended Through 15 March 2014) (Washington, D.C.: Joint Staff) p. 43.

28. B. H. Liddell Hart, *Strategy* (New York: Frederick A. Praeger, 1962) p. 24.

29. General Robert H. Barrow before the House of Representatives of the Commonwealth of Pennsylvania, 2 June 1981.

Printed in Great
Britain
by Amazon

31341551R00078